Please return this book on or before the due date below

The handbook has been devised to serve as a learning resource and a work of reference, with exercises, case studies, guidance and sources of information. I hope it will prove useful to those new to the role of managing volunteers and to those with experience. This book is primarily aimed at more formal volunteering opportunities. For many smaller, community-based, voluntary groups, implementing all the best practice approaches for managing volunteers could be 'mission impossible', but we hope that "The Volunteer Manager's Handbook" has some achievable ideas and valuable information for all volunteer-based projects.

Nicky McCrudden

It should be noted that any reference to legislation covering volunteering was correct at the time of publication.

Acknowledgement

The completion of this, my first book, is attributed to the support of many. Especially my husband Neil who gave me time, space and many cups of tea whilst I was working, and my parents, Robin and Babs who encourage and support me (emotionally and financially).

Particular thanks should also go to: Atiti Sosimi, who inspired and encouraged me to take the particular journey that I am on now; Mick Owen whose enthusiasm to publish this book pushed me to finish the project, and who no doubt spent many hours correcting my appalling spelling and grammar; and Katy Russell, my fellow 'novice' volunteer manager at the RNIB – and long-term sounding board!

The Volunteer Managers Handbook

Contents

One	Introduction	6
Two	Preparing to Involve Volunteers	13
Three	Volunteer Recruitment & Selection	21
Four	Managing Equalities in Volunteering	32
Five	Delivering Inductions & Developing Volunteers	40
Six	Managing Risks	44
Seven	Retaining & Rewarding Volunteers	54
Eight	Dealing with Problems & Ending Relationships	63

One: Introduction

This chapter takes a birds-eye view of the volunteering sector before considering the type of people who volunteer – their expectations, motivations, needs and skills - and then considers some of the factors that stop people volunteering.

As a volunteer manager, understanding what type of volunteer will be attracted to an opportunity is the first step in effective recruitment. Making assumptions about why people volunteer, or not even considering a volunteer's motivations are mistakes that will affect your ability to both recruit and retain them.

This chapter will encourage you to consider why people would give their time freely to your project, and will help you explore some of the barriers that organizations can inadvertently place in the way of potential volunteers.

The sector

People volunteer in all sorts of contexts. They can volunteer for statutory agencies such as local authorities, county councils, the police or NHS trusts and they can volunteer for not-for-profit groups such as national and local charities or community groups like sports clubs. Volunteering can be formal with a group or organization, or informal – keeping an eye on an older person who lives nearby, for example. Volunteering England reports that approximately 90 million hours of formal volunteering takes place weekly and that the economic value of that volunteering is around £40 billion per year.

Accurate data on volunteer-involving organizations is difficult to obtain because there is no single register. Many, but not all, are not-for-profit organizations which means that any profit made cannot be paid to individuals, but must be put into the organizations reserves, which in turn means that there is less need to register with a regulatory agency. The Charity Commission holds an ever-expanding list of charitable organizations, but not all volunteer-involving groups are registered. Many small community-based groups such as befriending schemes and local sports clubs, either do not view themselves as charities per se, or do not see the need to register.

The UK Voluntary Sector Almanacs 2006 and 2007, reported that:

- The not-for-profit sector has been expanding since 1991
- The majority of groups in the sector are smaller community-based groups, but over half have an income of less than £10,000 per annum
- As a result of the ever-increasing number of charities the sector's income has been rising in recent years, but incomes for each organization are more likely to be falling or remaining the same year-on-year.
- Although the not-for-profit sector is the only sector that receives voluntary income in the form of grants and donations, earned income is increasing in the sector. Income from donations is now most likely to be matched by selling goods or services; known as social enterprise.

- The number of people employed in the sector has dramatically increased from 483,000 employees in 1996 to 611,000 in 2005, and almost 40% of those workers are part-time. Voluntary and community groups employ more women (69% of the workforce) than men.

As for volunteer managers – around 84% of volunteer managers are in paid roles within the sector, but managing volunteers is usually a part of a broader job or role. There are very few people whose role is exclusively 'managing volunteers'.

Volunteers – worth their weight in gold

Volunteers can be so motivated and committed to a cause that they will turn up for 'work' come rain or shine, even though they are not being paid. The right volunteer recruited to the right role, and looked after well will not only be a motivated team member, but also a sterling advocate for your organization.

The traditional view of the volunteer as a retired person with a life-time of experience and time on their hands is slowly changing. There is a growing trend for younger people to be involved in volunteering and the 2005 Citizenship Survey suggested that 63% of 16-19 year olds volunteered at least once in twelve months, compared to 48% aged 50-64 years, and 50% of those aged 65-74.

It is difficult to have a single definition of a volunteer because not everyone who volunteers does so in the same way. Some people volunteer regularly with the same organization for years on end, others volunteer on an ad-hoc basis at events, and there are those who become a volunteer for just a short period of time.

One broad way to categorize volunteers is shown in the diagram below:

> **Stepping Stone Volunteers** have reached a turning point in their lives. They may be looking to return to work after a period of unemployment or ill health or they may be a student looking for experience for a CV. Whatever the reason, they see volunteering as stepping stone en route to their ultimate goal

> **Stalwart Volunteers** have a strong psychological investment to your organization's aims and objectives. They are very dedicated, passionate about your cause and volunteering is part of their identity. These are the type of volunteers who commit to a group long-term. In volunteer-led volunteering groups they are often the people that lead the project with their drive and passion.

> **Project Hopper Volunteers** move from one organization to another volunteering for limited periods. The classic example of this is a parent who volunteers while their children are involved in a particular sport or activity. Volunteering, and 'helping out' could be part of this person's mind set, but they'll probably enjoy short-term commitments on different projects.

As a volunteer manager, there is value in learning to recognise these different 'types' of volunteer, as they often benefit from slightly different management approaches. Knowing where a volunteer is 'coming from' can help a manager match them with the best role within a project. For example, a permanent role that requires a lot of input from a volunteer might not appeal to a Project Hopper, but might be well suited to a Stalwart and even a Stepping Stone Volunteer looking for that type of experience. Knowing the 'type' of volunteer you are working with may also influence the way you recognize their achievements. A Stepping Stone volunteer is likely to value certificates, awards and the offer of a reference to support their transition into a new life whilst it is not unknown for Stalwart volunteers to be offended by the offer of this type of external reward as theirs is a more intrinsic motivation see chapter 8.

Volunteer 'type' often influences the end of a volunteering relationship too. Stepping Stones are less likely to be with your project long-term. Once they have met their specific need, they may well move on. This is not a reflection on the organization or the volunteer manager – but do plan ahead for it. You will need to be ready to recruit to replace them one day. It is helpful to remember however that these categories are not set in stone, or mutually exclusive. An individual may be a Stalwart volunteer with one organization, but also a Project Hopper with other groups. A Stepping Stone Volunteer may become a long-term supporter if they are valued and treated well.

Individual motivations

Within these broad categories volunteers will have a great many specific, but different, reasons for getting involved.

Lisa's story will be familiar to many volunteer-based groups that provide services or activities for children. Lisa's youngest child had just started pre-school, and after the first week or so, she was accosted by one of the other parents looking for new members of the trustee committee. Not liking to say no too quickly, Lisa hesitated and was instantly 'signed-up'. In her heart she thought it was probably a good idea after all she was making sure the pre-school ran well for the sake of her daughter, and it wasn't really a big commitment. In essence, Lisa's motivation for volunteering, was to ensure a service existed for her daughter. There are many other reasons people give for becoming a volunteer:

meet new people	learn new skills
develop my CV	a route into work
committed to the cause	get recognition
use existing skills	fulfil an un-met need
because of a family member	give something back / do good
time on my hands	be part of a team
to get unique opportunities	build my confidence
experience something new	personal growth
have fun	sense of identity

Allan Luks, the author of "The Healing Power of Doing Good", provides evidence that suggests volunteering is just plain good for your health!

As a volunteer manager, knowing what motivates people is crucial in promoting your opportunity to potential volunteers, recruiting them to a role that can give them what they are looking for, managing their expectations and keeping them interested. But remember, motivation to a volunteer is not a fixed state; it can change over time. It did for Lisa. After two months the trustee committee's secretary stood down and Lisa took over the administration for them. She found she enjoyed the new challenge and her motivation shifted to learning skills to help her find a job. Sadly, no-one picked up on that shift in her reason for volunteering, and without the support she really wanted, Lisa stopped enjoying her volunteering and stood down.

Making the effort to find out why an individual wants to volunteer is time well spent. It is one of the most important questions to ask when recruiting potential volunteers (Chapter 3), and it is crucial that you monitor it during supervision (Chapter 7).

If volunteering is so great – why aren't we all doing it?

Just like Lisa, when volunteering is suggested to most people, their immediate and natural reaction is to rule themselves out – *"they won't be looking for someone like me"*. There are a variety of practical and psychological barriers that people put in the way of getting involved in volunteer work. Some are real, some are imagined. Organizations typically focus on tackling the practical issues; but research suggests that the psychological barriers are seen as more challenging to the potential volunteer. As a volunteer manager, one of your roles is to identify ALL the potential barriers to getting involved in your project. The National Occupational Standards for volunteer management highlight "reducing barriers to volunteering" as a key role for managers. Sometimes that might be as simple as helping potential volunteers see that these issues need not be a problem. Here are some of the most common barriers to volunteering and some ways to remove them:

Barrier	Volunteer managers can…
"I don't have enough time"	• Confirm the perception of the time involved. Include an estimated time involvement in publicity - but do not stipulate a minimum number of hours (see Chapter 2) • Be flexible – consider short-term volunteering, working from home, arranging hours to suit the volunteer, splitting roles, or using a rota
"I don't want to be labelled a do-gooder" or *"I'm not 'that' kind of person"*.	• Think carefully about the language used and images portrayed in your advertising and recruitment literature. • Make sure your organization's volunteers reflect the make-up of your local community by actively seeking to recruit a diverse range of volunteers (see chapter 4). • Emphasize the benefits that volunteers can get from joining your organization. Use existing volunteers as advocates (see Chap 3)
"I don't have the right skills"	• Highlight training opportunities (see Chapter 5) or get quotations from other volunteers about the skills they have learned since joining you.

"The recruitment process puts me off, I don't like forms"	• Make sure that applications and information are available in a variety of formats and support is available. • Make the recruitment process as informal as possible. • Ensure that you only ask potential volunteers for information that is relevant and necessary to the role.
"I'm not interested now my child is not involved"	• Try to continue the engagement at a time when the child is occupied doing whatever they have gone on to do. • Re-negotiate: offer the chance to stay on for a short-term basis or to volunteer for specific events. • Try and ensure that parent-volunteers get something from volunteering beyond supporting their child (see chapter 8)
"I receive state benefits and I'm worried that volunteering might affect the benefits that I get"	• Be aware of the rules on volunteering and benefits. For more information about volunteering whilst on benefits visit www.jobcentreplus.gov.uk
"I'm worried about having to have a Criminal Records Bureau (CRB) check"	• Make clear exactly when criminal checks are necessary for volunteers (see Chapter 6). • Be clear that the checks are to protect all concerned, including the volunteer • Make sure the project has an appropriate policy about the recruitment of ex-offenders and that it is given to any potential volunteers along with the application form.

Today's volunteer managers have a lot of responsibility in their organizations. Most of them are not full-time volunteer managers – it is just one part of another role. When you have recruitment worries and are concerned about the legalities of working with volunteers spending time getting to know them can seem like a fairly low priority. However, most grass-roots services only exist because of volunteers and volunteers are people with their own motivations and needs. Making an effort to uncover and support those needs is one easy way to prolong volunteering relationships; or at the very least ensure that when your volunteers leave you they tell everyone they know how great volunteering for you is!

Exercise:

1. Think about the people who volunteer for your organization. Make a note of the characteristics of each.

2. What 'types' of volunteers seem to be attracted to your organization?

3. Why do you think that is?

4. Do you need to do something about this?

Two: Preparing to Involve Volunteers

Is every role appropriate for a volunteer? In some cases, there is no other choice. Sport in the UK is a good example of that - most grass roots clubs depend entirely on volunteer coaches and committee members - and many community art projects rely on volunteer drivers, administrators and so on.

In other cases the decision is whether an opportunity is suitable for a volunteer, or should be undertaken by an employee.

But how should an organization, whether it is a small community group, or a statutory agency, prepare for volunteer involvement. This chapter looks at planning to involve volunteers, including the policies and paperwork that must be and should be in place, and gives practical tips on creating those documents.

A role for volunteers or staff?

The first question to answer is, "is this role something that a volunteer should be doing, or should it be done by a paid member of staff?" For small community groups like Sunday League football clubs this is an easy decision – everyone fulfils their role on a voluntary basis. Distinguishing whether roles are most appropriate for volunteers or for paid workers is not so easy for larger charities, or for statutory organizations.

Although there are no strict rules for deciding whether a role is suitable for a volunteer, Volunteering England offer some guidance. Volunteers should not be recruited for work that is so monotonous or unattractive that paid workers just don't want to do it. In truth, long-term retention of volunteers for uninspiring work can be hard; after all, there is no financial incentive. And it won't help the reputation of your group in the volunteering world if volunteers are only offered jobs that no-one else wants. Equally, volunteers should not be used to replace, or do the same work as, existing paid staff. The emergency services in the UK illustrate this point well. Ambulance Trusts recruit 'Community Responders' – volunteers trained to respond to medical emergencies in their local community before full-time ambulance crews can reach them. Community Responders provide basic life support; they do not undertake the same role as paramedics. Their role is to support the work of paid ambulance staff. The Fire Service has retained fire-fighters, members of the public with other vocations, who in an emergency fulfil the role of fire-fighter. Retained fire-fighters undertake a role equal to that of their full-time colleagues, they handle emergencies and will cover for full-time crews when resources are committed to a large scale emergency. Community Responders are volunteers, they do not replace paid staff. Retained fire-fighters, receive a payment (a retainer), and are not volunteers because they do exactly the same jobs as paid staff.

Based on the Volunteering England guidance, the checklist below will help you consider if the role you are thinking of is suitable for a volunteer:

- Is the role something that a volunteer might want to do?
- Is it sufficiently interesting to maintain a volunteer's motivation?

- Is the level of responsibility involved, e.g. for budget or people management, appropriate for a volunteer?
- What training or other investment must the organization make to get the volunteer started?
- Are there, or has there recently been, paid staff doing this work?
- Is there any risk to the organization, should the volunteer leave suddenly?
- Is there anything else that suggests that this role should be done by someone who is paid?

Having policies in place to support volunteering

Once you have decided to involve volunteers in your organization, there are a range of policies and documents that you should have ready. The number and types of policies will vary depending on the nature of the group or organization. Informal volunteering is just that, informal, and groups are unlikely to see the need for detailed policies. However, clear statements and agreed principles on key issues will help to set the parameters under which volunteers are involved, help manage risk (see Chapter 6) and help ensure decisions are made equitably (see Chapter 9).

For larger organizations, a wide range of policies should already be in place. These should apply equally to volunteers, but it can be advisable to make a clear distinction between paid staff and volunteers when applying policies. Having separate policies for volunteers helps to distinguish volunteers from employees, and reinforces the flexIbility of the rolo of volunteers. In some policies, that may simply mean changing the word 'employees' to 'volunteers' and reprinting the document.

Below is a check-list of some of the policies that volunteer-involving organizations may need to have. Many of these can be as complex or as simple as the organization wishes to make them.

Role description	All volunteer-involving organizations, even small community groups should have a basic role description for each volunteering role. (see below)
Volunteer agreement	Outlines what the organization and the volunteer might reasonably expect from one another. This short document should exist in any volunteer-involving organization (see below).
Volunteering policy	A statement about the nature of your group which distinguishes volunteers from paid staff. Most relevant to larger organizations that have employees and volunteers.
Ex-offenders policy	Wherever an organization is obliged to conduct CRB checks on potential volunteers (see Chapter 6) that group must have a policy regarding the recruitment of ex-offenders. The policy should welcome applications from a wide range of potential volunteers and explain why checks are needed. It should contain a statement about the confidentiality of criminal disclosures and a promise of fair treatment. This policy should be a standard part of application packs wherever CRB checks are required.

Insurance	Every volunteer-involving organization should have an insurance policy that covers volunteers (see Chapter 6).
Equal opportunities policy	Having an equal opportunities policy commits an organization to treating everyone fairly and is good practice for all volunteer-involving organizations. It is not a legal requirement, but some funders expect organizations to have this kind of statement (see Chapter 4).
Health and safety policy	Although they represent good practice, health and safety policies are usually only found in larger volunteer-involving organizations. Policies for employees can easily be adapted for volunteers.
Risk management	All organizations working with volunteers have a duty of care to assess the risks to those volunteers and take steps to reduce any possible harm (see Chapter 6).
Accident /injury report form	Every organization should have a place to log details of accidents, injuries or serious illness. In accordance with Data Protection legislation this should not be a book, but loose leaflet reports that once completed should be stored securely in a locked cabinet. Such forms can be purchased from most stationary suppliers.
Safeguarding and protecting children policy	This should exist for any organization that engages with young people at any time either as members or as service users.

Data protection and confidentiality	Every volunteer-involving organization will hold personal information about its volunteers and therefore should be aware of the terms of the Data Protection Act (see Chapter 6).

Some organizations will also need to consider the confidentiality of information about service users. Volunteers working in an advice centre, for example, may have access to confidential information about clients, and may be asked to sign a confidentially agreement. |
Reimbursement of expenses policy and claim form	Wherever a volunteer-involving organization has a budget, reimbursing out-of-pocket expenses is a fundamental element of good practice. Volunteers should find it easy to know what they can claim for and how to do so.
Problem solving process	The way that volunteers can lodge a complaint, and the way problems with volunteers are handled should be clearly set out. It is good practice, and reassuring for volunteers, to know that the organization has a procedure in place for dealing with grievances. This does not have to be a long and complex document (see Chapter 8).
Code of Conduct	Because of the nature of their core activity some organizations find it helpful to set out a code of conduct for volunteers. This is certainly true of sports coaches, for example. The contents of the code might include guidance on appearance/dress code, reliability, language and any behaviour considered to be gross mis-conduct (that would lead to instant dismissal of the volunteer). Where appropriate, volunteers may be asked to sign copies of the code to indicate that they have read and understand the code.

Volunteer role descriptions

A role description provides an outline of how you want to involve volunteers. A role description should be created for **every** volunteer position regardless of the size of the group or level of formality. Specifying the role, the knowledge, experience and the skills required for a volunteering position is an element of the NOS for volunteer management.

Some organizations prefer to develop role descriptions around an individual volunteer's skills, arguing that this gives a more inclusive approach to volunteers. However, if you do not know what you want a volunteer to do, how can you recruit effectively? Some roles have unavoidable requirements. If you are running a 'buddy scheme' that requires volunteers to provide transport for disabled gym users, for example, you cannot escape the necessary qualification of 'clean driving licence'. Any initial ambiguity about what you need from volunteers will also hamper your ability to retain them. Detailed role descriptions are especially important if you intend to recruit via a third party, such as www.do-it.org.uk, or a local volunteer centre, as they will not have your understanding of the volunteering opportunity to brief potential volunteers.

The role description gives clear and concise details of:

- All the tasks a volunteer is expected to be involved in,
- How often a volunteer might need to be available,
- What, if any skills are essential
- How they will be supported, supervised and trained.

Creating a role description also helps volunteer managers to clarify the role they think they need and to assess their capacity to supervise and support a volunteer. Once completed, it will help to identify what type of volunteer they are looking for; do they need someone short-term with certain skills in place or someone who is willing to train?

On the other side of the equation, a well-constructed role description will help potential volunteers match their own skills and background to that required in the role. And the role description means that the volunteering opportunity can be openly advertised and the description given with any other useful information to appropriate potential volunteers.

Below is list of headings and questions that may help to create a comprehensive role description. Remember, just like you a volunteer may be looking for a sense of achievement and pride in what they are doing. Try and avoid assigning all the menial jobs to a volunteer role.

Role Title:

Avoid vague terms like 'Volunteer Role Description'. Each role should have a title that is inspiring, or at least descriptive.

Purpose of the role

What type of work does it involve?

Key activities

What are the main tasks, and what activities are involved in completing these? Is there any flexibility in any parts of the role?

What responsibility will they have? Will they be responsible for other people such as other volunteers, children or vulnerable adults)?

Are there any team meetings, committee meetings or other meetings you would like them to attend)?

Experience, skills and/or qualifications

What personal qualities are important; communicator, enthusiastic, organised?

Be sensible about what you require; asking for a degree will exclude lots of potential volunteers. But be realistic; a children's sports coach should have an appropriate qualification, a CRB check and perhaps first aid. Identify those qualities that are essential before appointment and those you can help them work towards.

The practicalities

Where will they be based? Usual time involvement: how long do you need them for, how often, are there set days and times? Who will they be working with?

Is there any requirement for screening: references, criminal background checks, approval by the Independent Safeguarding Authority (ISA)?

The benefits

What expenses are you able to pay? How and when do you pay them? Remember that not everyone has a bank account, or can afford to wait for monthly expenses.

Is there training available? What other benefits can you offer: parking, transport, refreshments,

references?
Support provided
Who are they responsible to? What supervision will they get? How would they make a complaint?
For more information
Who should they contact?

Once you complete this exercise you need to evaluate the role and decide whether the role could be shared between more than one volunteer or divided to allow you to accept a volunteer who does not have all the skills. Finally, take an objective look at the role description to make sure it clearly makes the role a volunteering one and not a paid job.

Volunteer managers must be very careful to avoid inferring a contract of employment within role descriptions. If employed status is inadvertently suggested the organization may be liable to pay the national minimum wage, backdated wages and potentially a criminal fine. Avoid using contractual language, such as 'job', 'payment' or 'work', in role descriptions and putting too many obligations on your volunteers. In particular, do not enforce minimum time commitments from volunteers – it implies a duty. It is, however, acceptable to suggest a 'usual minimum involvement' but there should be no sanctions for those who do not give the 'usual minimum' amount of time. Role descriptions and volunteer agreements should refer to 'reasonable expectations' and not 'commitments'.

Remember, a role description is a living document. After your volunteer has been recruited and is in post, the role description should be re-visited at regular intervals to ensure it remains a true reflection of the role that volunteer fulfils. Add a review date, and the person responsible for reviewing the document to the bottom, to make sure that the review happens.

Volunteer policies and agreements

A volunteer policy defines the general nature of the relationship between the volunteer and the organization. It can usually be achieved on one side of A4. Volunteer policies are not specific to individual roles, they simply outline the broad values and principles of your group, and where appropriate offer a distinction between volunteers and paid staff. In larger organizations volunteer policies can signpost to other policies that apply to volunteers like the grievance procedure, health and safety policy and so on. Again, managers should take steps to avoid inferring a contractual relationship when writing or reviewing policies.

Volunteer agreements detail what volunteers and organizations can expect from one another. This might include such things as a request that volunteers respect confidentiality, adhere to safety guidelines, attend meetings and necessary training and give as much notice as possible if they decide not to volunteer. In return the volunteer can expect an induction, training, fair treatment, reimbursement of out-of-pocket expenses and so on. It is advisable to state within volunteer agreements that there is no intention to create a legally binding contract or a contract of employment. Finally, avoid asking volunteers to sign the agreement, as it could suggest an attempt at 'binding'. An example of a volunteer agreement is shown below.

> **Sample volunteer agreement**
>
> This agreement sets out what volunteers can expect from *(organization's name)*, and what we hope for from our volunteers. Volunteers are an important and valuable part of our organization and we hope that volunteers enjoy their time with us.
>
> *(Organization name)* hopes:
>
> - to welcome you with enough information about the organization and your role within it
> - to provide an accurate role description and any training you may need to volunteer
> - to allow you time to meet with *(managers name or role)* to make sure things are going well for both us and you, that your role description reflects what you are doing and let you know what is happening in the organization
> - to respect your skills, dignity and individual wishes and to do our best to meet them
> - to pay any out-of-pocket expenses *(describe the type of expenses paid, or sign post to the appropriate document for more information)*
> - to provide a safe environment to volunteer in and make sure you are insured appropriately
> - to apply our equal opportunities, health and safety, complaints/grievance and confidentially policies to all our volunteers.
>
> As a volunteer, I agree to do my best:
>
> - to volunteer reliably to the best of my ability, and to give as much warning as possible whenever I cannot volunteer when expected
> - to follow *(organization name)* rules and procedures, including its health and safety policy, its equal opportunities policy, the relevant code of conduct and its confidentiality policy.
>
> This agreement is in honour only. It is not intended to be legally binding, and *(organization name)* in no way intends to create a contract of employment with our volunteers.

Much of the paperwork associated with contemporary volunteer management is viewed by managers as onerous and off-putting, but with many websites offering sample policies and statements it need not be (see Further Help). Having appropriate policies in place can reassure volunteers that the organization takes their involvement and support seriously, and can help to reduce the likelihood of problems in the long-run. Once completed and approved by a trustee board or other appropriate forum, volunteers should be introduced to policies or guidelines as part of their induction (see Chapter 5).

Three: Volunteer Recruitment & Selection

Volunteering England reports that 95% of volunteer-involving organizations still rely on word of mouth as their primary means of recruiting volunteers. This approach limits your potential volunteer pool to those in the social circles of those already involved.

In my first volunteer management role, I rapidly learned that attending community events and fairs can translate into one or two volunteers if you're lucky. But strategic recruitment can save wasted time and help you to get motivated and committed volunteers from the outset. Then a colleague asked how I selected volunteers. I looked back at her with some confusion – this implied I might reject some volunteers. Why would I do that? I now understand that selection is very much part of volunteer management.

Chapter 1 looked at the motivations of volunteers. Chapter 2 explored the requirements of the organization. Chapter 3 matches these two needs as part of the process of volunteer recruitment and selection.

Effective recruitment begins with having a strong role description (see Chapter 2). After all, how can you ask someone to undertake a voluntary role, if you don't know what it is you need them to do? Recruitment is hard work and often your efforts won't be rewarded straight away. Some potential volunteers will hold on to a leaflet for weeks and even months and get in touch when the time is right for them.

Recruitment of volunteers is not like recruiting to a paid post, primarily because you cannot offer any reward either financial or non-financial. But that is not to say that you cannot provide incentives. Remember Lisa from Chapter 1? Lisa gave up volunteering for a pre-school committee because she did not feel she was really learning new skills that would help her back into work after being a full-time mother. She later became the secretary for a rugby club that her brother played for because they promised to help her develop just those skills. The out-going secretary spent time with Lisa showing her the ropes, and then the club paid for her to go on a short course on minuting meetings with their local Council for Voluntary Service (CVS). That in itself was enough incentive for Lisa, but being invited to the club dinner-dance and the offer of a reference didn't hurt either! A great example of the incentives that can be offered to persuade someone to volunteer.

It can take a lot of effort to attract just one volunteer, and it will not always be the 'right' potential volunteer that finds a path to your door! But there are things you can do to improve your chances of getting the right volunteers.

The National Survey of Volunteering revealed that one of the most important reasons why people do not volunteer is a lack of information on volunteering opportunities; they simply had never been asked. Lisa found out about the opportunity at the rugby club by word of mouth, but that is a very limiting way of finding new volunteers. Advertising and promotion increases your chances of recruiting a volunteer and of recruiting a diverse range of volunteers (see Chapter 4), but avoid the clichéd "volunteers needed" unless you are an established and well-known charity; it doesn't say what you are looking for and it is unlikely to inspire anyone.

Volunteer managers trying to recruit, often find that many potential volunteers deselect themselves: "I can't do that", "They'd want someone with experience" yourself, so the actual recruitment message must be powerful. When writing an advertisement, use plain English and avoid phrases, like 'gym buddy' that might not mean much to people outside a narrow field. One way of writing an advertisement is to start with a 'call to action' inspiring potential volunteers to respond; we all like to feel that what we are being asked to do is valuable. Follow this with a clear image of how *they* can help tackle the problem. Without misrepresenting the role emphasise the positive elements and highlight the way the opportunity links with the motivations of potential volunteers to help (see Chapter 1). Finally, address at least one of the potential barriers (see Chapter 1). McCurley and Linch in their American publication, Essential Volunteer Management, give a good example of this approach.

> **CHILDREN ARE BEING ABUSED**
>
> You can help them by offering temporary shelter.
>
> We'll show you how you can help these children and help yourself at the same time.
>
> Call .....

Where and how to advertise for volunteers

Often one exposure to a request for help will not prompt potential volunteers into action. A potential volunteer may see an advertisement once and think about the opportunity. The second time they see it, they will remember thinking it was interesting. The third time they might follow it up. The clever recruiter will employ more than one recruitment strategy in a relatively short time frame so maximising their impact on their target audience.

There are essentially two approaches to recruiting volunteers, blanket and targeted. Blanket recruitment casts the net as wide as possible with the message heard by a wide audience. It includes leaflet drops, posters, newspaper advertisements, radio appeals, and stands at events. It is an ideal approach:

- where lots of volunteers are needed, or
- for roles that don't need specialist skills or
- for roles that anyone can be trained to do.

The drive for volunteers for the London Olympics is a good example of blanket recruitment. Options for blanket recruitment include:

Leaflets: These can be mass produced relatively cost-effectively these days and can be designed to appeal to particular groups. For example images of young people playing football would work if you were looking to target people with a passion for the sport to coach a team. Leaflets can be distributed to wide variety of places including job centres, libraries, chambers of commerce, educational establishments, youth clubs, health centres, community centres, volunteer centres in fact anywhere there is a waiting room. But don't just think about the places that you go to.

Newspapers: If you're going to advertise in newspapers, think carefully about what section you place your advertisement in. Who reads the 'Jobs' page of local newspapers? If you are going to run advertisements here make sure they spell out the potential for gaining relevant work experience, but make it clear it is a voluntary post. A Citizens Advice Bureau in the south of England used to regularly place advertisements in the jobs section of a local paper and kept getting calls from people who had misunderstood and thought paid posts were available. When placing advertisements in newspapers remember, every form of media has a type of readership. If you think your opportunity is ideally suited to young people volunteering in the summer holidays, placing an advertisement in a paper mainly read by older people is not going to be very effective.

Human interest story: It can be more effective to get a journalist to present a human interest story. A town athletics club recruited two new volunteers when the local paper ran a story about a successful local athlete thanking their volunteer coach and ended the story with details of how others could get involved with volunteering. These often attract more media interest if they coincide with a relevant national or international campaign. A diary of events is available at www.countmeincalendar.info

Volunteering events and fairs: These are run in some areas, but are most often frequented by individuals who already volunteer. Events such as these are great for networking with other volunteering organizations but if you are trying to recruit your message may easily be lost among the dozens of other groups looking for volunteers.

Displays at public venues: It is far better to try and get a public display at a venue where you will not be expected and competition is low such as your local supermarket, a summer fayre or freshers' events at universities. Ideally, involve an existing volunteer as their motives are often see as purer than paid staff and have your stand during the hours you want people to volunteer. If they are at the supermarket at that time, then it is likely to be their free time!

The internet: Many organizations use the internet to recruit volunteers. Perhaps the most well known of these opportunities is www.do-it.org, but other sites also exist including www.timebank.org.uk and www.csv.org.uk. More general websites and social networking sites such as Facebook can also be used effectively to raise the profile of your organization. Or you can develop your own site; if you don't have the necessary skill-set, consider recruiting an IT skilled volunteer.

What if the role you are looking to fill requires more definite skill-sets, involves monotonous tasks or might be daunting to potential volunteers such as working with a client group perceived as dangerous or unsavoury? Targeted recruitment means being more specific about who you ask to volunteer. It might involve:

- using your role description to ask who might want to do that role; young/old, male/female, professional/skilled.

- identifying people who already work in a particular field; asking a specialist homeless health worker to train as a sports coach for a project to provide physical activity opportunities for homeless people

- approach individuals directly affected by the cause such as former clients and their families.

If you already have volunteers doing that role assess whether there is anything common to them all. Are they all parents? Do they all come from the same background? Then apply your recruitment efforts to areas where those types of people will be. If you are looking for race marshals, try linking with athletics clubs; if you need people to register large numbers of participants recruit the reception team from your local GP surgery or a big hotel.. Don't forget existing volunteers can be invaluable in recruiting. Why not encourage them to bring a friend or family member along to a session, or social. Other options include:

Specialist publications: This type of advertising can be costly, but you could try appealing to publication editors for 'distressed space' (unsold advertising space). These type of publications generally have a smaller readership but if you are looking for someone with a financial background to lead a debit advice service, magazines especially for financial advisers get your message directly to your target audience.

Giving talks to groups: Talks have the advantage of offering two-way communication. Groups might be those who regularly get involved in helping the community such as the Womens Institute and Rotary clubs, or those whose members you have targeted as likely to be interested in your cause. Involving an existing volunteer in the presentation can be very powerful, especially if the audience can identify with that person; but it is important that someone present can answer questions about the organization and the role you are trying to fill. During the presentation, highlight the barriers and counter them and make sure you clearly **ask** for volunteers. If possible do not rush off after your talk; many people prefer to talk one-to-one.

Strategic partnerships: Aligning your organization with local agencies is a great way to recruit new volunteers. The R.N.I.B.'s project empowering visually impaired adults to engage with sport and leisure recruited volunteers via a local university which had a large sports studies department. Many universities have a volunteer brokerage service, as do County Sports Partnerships and many areas have Volunteer Centres aligned to the area's Council for Voluntary Service (CVS).

Even opportunities that could appeal to a broad spectrum of the population can benefit from some targeting. The motivations of young, old and middle-aged people are unlikely to be the same but if you are looking for volunteer tour guides for your museum emphasize work experience to the younger audience and social interaction to the older groups. By doing this you increase the likely number of expressions of interest from each demographic.

Employer supported volunteering (ESV)

There is an existing national campaign called Time To Give Time and a growing trend for employers across all sectors to support and encourage volunteering. This ranges from basic support such as allowing staff who already volunteer to fund raise at work, or make use of the photocopier to releasing staff on paid sabbaticals to undertake voluntary work. A construction firm that built schools initiated a scheme where its construction staff went back to the schools they had built and helped the children learn to read. By all accounts it was a scheme genuinely valued by the firm's staff and an increasing number of organizations are seeing that allowing their people to undertake voluntary work can form part of a training programme, can increase the organization's community profile, can improve staff the motivation and gives those that volunteer an insight into the needs of their 'customers'. As a form of recruitment it could be worth approaching local employers or the Chamber of Commerce to suggest strategic partnerships to develop ESV.

If some is good, more must be better

It is common for volunteer managers to think it is a good thing to have lots of potential volunteers, but this is not the best approach. The 1997 National Survey of Volunteering showed that potential volunteers are put off by delays. If you keep potential volunteers waiting because you only have one vacancy they are likely to find another opportunity. Worse still is to accept the services of all those who are interested if you do not have enough for them to do! Another concern is not having enough of the 'right' volunteers, or too many of the 'wrong' volunteers. Not all volunteers are suited to every role (see Chapter 4) so appropriate recruitment and selection is important. Before you start recruiting know how many of what type of person you need to fulfil what roles!

Whichever approach you use to recruit new volunteers, make sure you are prepared for enquiries. Nothing will irritate a potential volunteer more than not being able to find out what they need to know and with so many other options for volunteering you could lose them before you have even begun. Always have information packs and application forms ready and waiting. Where the role could be seen as boring, firstly consider combining it with more exciting activities. If that really isn't an option, then recruitment should emphasize how the role matches volunteers motivations – stuffing envelops can be done in a social environment, or at a time to suit.

Exercise:

1. Does the volunteer role require specialist skills or could almost anyone doe it, albeit with a little training?

2. What type of person would enjoy the role?

3. What type of recruitment strategy would suit your role best?

4. If your role requires certain skills:

    a) where can you find these sorts of people? Where do they shop? what groups or professional societies do they belong to? Where do they worship?

    b) is there anything that existing volunteers have in common? do they share an interest in drama? Do they have the same educational background? Do they live near each other?

Should you interview volunteers?

As well as volunteers' time, a considerable amount of the manager's time will be invested in inducting, supporting and supervising volunteers. If the volunteers are not well matched to their role more time will be needed to recruit again; or worse deal with numerous problems and complaints from the volunteer. Helping a potential volunteer to assess their own suitability for a volunteering opportunity is part of the NOS.

Interviewing volunteers is one way to demonstrate that their involvement is taken seriously. According to the Institute for Volunteering Research, around 84% of volunteer-involving organizations hold an interview or informal chat with volunteers before they start their role. However it is not clear how many of these use this chat for screening and selection.

Even informal 'getting to know each other' chats with potential new volunteers should have a purpose and structure and there is a sample first meeting structure below. It is a chance for the volunteer manager to find out the potential volunteer's expectations and their motivations for volunteering (see Chapter 1). Where the volunteer's aims fit with the organization's and the role under discussion the relationship will flourish. Where there is a mismatch the volunteer may feel misled, disenchanted and not committed to your group. A volunteer who is not getting what they need, or want, from volunteering is unlikely to be motivated, could be less than reliable and is not going to be committed to you in the long term.

> At the first meeting with a volunteer applying to support adults with severe learning difficulties participating in craft activities it became clear that the potential volunteer was anticipating that they would join in the class themselves.
>
> The volunteer manager carefully explained to the potential volunteer that the role essentially involved a lot of caring for the scheme beneficiaries and most volunteers did not have time to participate in craft classes themselves. For this reason the volunteer manager was concerned that the volunteer would not fully enjoy the opportunity.
>
> The potential volunteer was asked if they would like some more time to think about volunteering, or to come along and watch a class. They declined, but thanked the volunteer manager for being so candid with them.

The level of formality you use will depend entirely on your organization. For the majority of volunteer-involving organizations, informality is the watch-word. A brief chat over coffee helps both parties decide if they would like to proceed. For some of the larger charities who attract lots of interest from volunteers a competitive interview might be the only realistic approach to selection. Either way it is worth inviting an existing volunteer to come along too; they are much more likely to understand what it feels like to be a new volunteer and the potential volunteer is less likely to be intimidated by another volunteer.

Interviews can take place in many different locations:

- the place the volunteering takes place which will help to familiarize the new volunteer with the venue

- in a coffee shop; very relaxed and informal, but it can be difficult for the potential volunteer to raise any personal or sensitive matters

- in the potential volunteer's home. The potential volunteer is likely to feel much more relaxed and if required filling out CRB forms can be easier as all the information is to hand, but it can leave the volunteer manager vulnerable if they are a lone worker.

Wherever you choose to interview potential volunteers, the venue should be accessible and ideally near to public transport.

It is worth having a basic framework for your interview to make sure you do not miss out any important information. (See the exercise at the end of the chapter). The meeting should be very much a two-way process – a chance to see if the skills, experience and motivations of the volunteer match those of the opportunity available. Potential volunteers should be given enough information about the organization and the role - hours of volunteering, level of involvement, level of support, details of reimbursement of expenses, training and recognition - to decide if they would like to proceed. Some organizations use the first meeting as an opportunity to complete an application form together. Smaller groups might shy away from application forms; but they are part of best practice and at their simplest they provide a good way of ensuring you record all the relevant information from potential volunteers.

At the first meeting managers should be seeking to understand the potential volunteer's motivations by asking a range of open-ended questions about what they hope to get out of their volunteering and what attracted them to the organization. The answers should enable both parties to reflect on whether their needs will be satisfied in the relationship. Remember, although they are not applying for a paid job, equality issues still apply in volunteer interviews. Questions relating to age, marital status, religion, nation of origin and sexual preference are not appropriate. However this type of meeting does allow the volunteer manager to assess the attitudes of potential volunteers around the organization's core principles. For example if your school walking bus scheme is in an area with a diverse ethnic mix of children you may want to assess the potential volunteer's views on racial equality.

An example of a template for a first meeting with potential volunteers is shown below.

Template for a first meeting with potential volunteers

1. Welcome the potential volunteer to the meeting. Make clear to them the purpose of the meeting.

2. Explain how long the meeting will take and what you hope to gain from it - giving and receiving information, discussing any issues or concerns that they may have, allow both parties to decide if they would like to proceed.

3. Seek information from the volunteer. Questions might include: what attracted them to the role, what are their interests and experiences, what would they like to get from it, how much time do they think they would like to give, is there anything that concerns them about volunteering, what do they understand about the organization?

4. Provide the potential volunteer with information about the organization and its purpose. Tell them about the activities and practicalities, expectations, expenses, available support, training, benefits of volunteering and time commitment of the role.

5. Discuss any specialist skills required or any challenging aspects of the role.

6. Try to reach a mutual decision about whether the potential volunteer would still like to join the organization. Clarify what happens next and if necessary complete an application form and CRB form with the volunteer.

7. If possible, offer to pay out of pocket expenses for attending the meeting.

After the meeting – send for references and ensure that confidential information is stored securely.

Making a decision

Not every potential volunteer will be suited to your role and there are a range of tools to help volunteer managers match volunteers and opportunities. Often potential volunteers will deselect themselves if your opportunity does not seem to give them what they are looking for. Tools available to the volunteer manager include CRB checks where one is relevant to the role and references.

Potential volunteers should ideally supply two references who are not relatives. Some small groups may not see this as necessary, but it should form part of a risk management process (see Chapter 6) and can be used to ask referees to confirm their knowledge, skills and qualities appropriate to the role. A reference might be a telephone conversation, a 'tick box form' or a request for a letter of reference; but confidentiality should be emphasized to the referee. Some potential volunteers may find it difficult to give two references – asylum seekers for example. Volunteer managers should be prepared for this and have an agreed approach to volunteers who cannot supply references such as taking them on in a supervised role for a period of time.

Where the volunteering role brings volunteers into close contact with children and 'vulnerable' individuals, an enhanced criminal record bureau (CRB) check becomes an essential part of the selection process. A 'vulnerable' person is anyone under 18 years of age, any individual with substantial physical, sensory or learning disability, physical or mental illness (including substance addictions), or those with a reduction of mental or physical capacity due to advanced years. Any volunteer offering personal care as part of their role – such as 'gym buddies' who help people get changed - must also be screened. However, it is not appropriate to apply for an enhanced CRB check for volunteers not working with these client groups and collecting the information would be deemed to be excessive and therefore, under the terms of the data protection act, likely to be illegal.

If a CRB check is required it is good practice to inform potential volunteers at the application stage, as well as to provide a copy of your policy on ex-offenders (see Chapter 2). Though the actual CRB check is free for volunteers, some smaller voluntary groups cannot afford the fee to register as an organization approved to carry out checks. Some CVSs, local authorities and sports governing bodies provide a CRB checking service although they may charge a fee for the administration involved in processing the form. It can take a number of weeks after submitting the form before the disclosure is received. In that period, volunteer managers should not allow new volunteers to work with children or vulnerable adults.

If a disclosure is returned with convictions on it is worth remembering that approximately a quarter of the working age population has a criminal conviction, so that should not instantly exclude potential volunteers. Volunteer managers need to base decisions about whether to accept volunteers with convictions on:

- the type of offence; some offences bar people from working with children and vulnerable adults

- the date and relevance of convictions,

- any pattern of offending,

- the potential volunteer's explanation, and

- other references.

Tempting as it might be to want to discuss the situation with other members of your team, remember, it is illegal to disclose details of convictions to others without the individual's consent! If you want to talk to colleagues, you should first ask for the potential volunteer's agreement. (More information on CRB checks and disclosures can be found in chapter 6).

However, from late 2009 this decision making process will be taken on by the Independent Safeguarding Authority (ISA). Where relevant, volunteers must hold ISA approval. Organisations will simply be advised whether, or not, the volunteer is suitable to work with children or vulnerable adults. Volunteer managers will no longer be responsible for making that decision.

Rejecting potential volunteers

To involve a volunteer when the volunteer manager is unsure whether they are well-matched to the group is unfair to both the organization and to the potential volunteer. It would be counter-productive as the likelihood is the group would not retain the volunteer and the individual's experience of the voluntary sector could be tainted permanently. Where the volunteer is not thought to be suited to the opportunity, or for legal reasons is not permitted to volunteer in the role, the manager should offer positive feedback, say why they feel the volunteer would not feel fulfilled in that role, or encourage them to reflect on that themselves and refer them to alternative sources of volunteering opportunities.

Finally; your role description, appropriate recruitment strategy and well-structured first meeting with potential volunteers should help them to assess their own suitability for a role. Where a potential volunteer is not suited to the role that they applied for the NOS for Volunteer Managers requires the manager to refer them to alternative volunteering opportunities. The best way to do this is via your local Volunteer Centre, or the do-it website.

Exercise:

1. What information would potential volunteers find helpful to know about the role and about your organization?

2. What do you want to know about their motivations, skills, experience and availability?

3. Are there any attitudes or views that you would like to explore with potential volunteers?

4. Would it be helpful to know about any extra support needs the potential volunteer may have?

Four: Managing Equality in Volunteering

"All people in the world should have the right to freely offer their time, talent and energy to others and to their communities."

Universal declaration on volunteering (International Association of Volunteer Effort, 2001)

Many smaller volunteering organizations recruit new volunteers by word of mouth alone. Although cost-effective, this severely limits the 'pool' from which new volunteers can be drawn. Think of the local football team that relies on former players volunteering. Not only does this limit their potential volunteers to those immediately within the social circles of their members, it also raises the question of how well their club reflects the community it represents.

For some people a chapter on equality might typify what they see as the over formalization of volunteering but not only is equality a moral issue, in today's world it is often a requirement of funders.

Your volunteers should reflect the differences within your local community. Groups that have sought to achieve that have found that people move towards their organization more readily. Not just volunteers but service users also have increased faith that the organization understands their needs.

Sue was happy to take her daughter Karlie to the drama club at the local community trust because of the people she saw involved in the club. "Karlie, is profoundly deaf and perhaps I'm an overprotective mum, but I worry about her at after-school clubs. I just felt that the trust would understand. One of the group's helpers has Downs Syndrome and they are great with him, so I felt reassured that she'd be looked after." Sue had faith that the club would be welcoming and ready to understand her daughter needs, because she saw the needs of others being met.

Apart from increasing the number of people joining your club, or using your service, and being an appropriate way to behave in a modern society, other benefits of inclusive volunteering include:

- increasing the number of possible volunteers you can recruit and therefore improving your chances of finding the 'right' volunteer for the role;

- generating a wider range of ideas - a more diverse group of volunteers is likely to be more creative in their thinking;

- better motivation and retention of volunteers: evidence from employment situations shows inclusive organizations retain motivated staff for longer. There is every reason to expect this to apply equally to managing volunteers;

- protecting your organization from claims of discrimination. An organization does not have to be intentionally discriminating to break the law; discrimination can be direct, indirect, accidental or even arise from well-intentioned actions. Reviewing the equality approach of your organization is an important step to avoid unintentional discrimination (see below); and

- improving your chances of getting funding. Many funders require organizations to provide evidence of inclusive volunteering.

> *"Equality matters to the Big Lottery Fund. We want to use lottery money to bring about changes to communities by funding people, projects and programmes with a particular emphasis on community needs. This (guide) is part of our drive to promote equality and maximise opportunities for people to take part in the projects we fund. By putting equality right at the heart of project design and implementation, organizations are more likely to achieve better outcomes."*
>
> The Big Lottery: Equality Matters Guidance

Finally, if a volunteer manager is delivering a project as a sub-contractor of a statutory agency such as a local authority, an NHS trust or the police they may be legally required to operate at the same standard of equality imposed on statutory bodies.

But the voluntary sector is already good at equality, isn't it? Whilst it is true that the voluntary and community sector is the largest employer of disabled workers in 1999 the Trades Union Congress (TUC) reported that 19% of the support they gave to gay and lesbian workers experiencing discrimination was to individuals in the voluntary sector. It is too easy for some voluntary and community groups to assume an understanding of equality. The RAISE Equalities Toolkit cites details of a small group set up by the parents of disabled children who were turned down by a funder for a grant because they did not have an equal opportunities policy and could not provide evidence of their inclusiveness. An "instinctive approach to equal opportunities" was not sufficient, and although they had a clear understanding of disability issues, they failed to take account of other disadvantaged groups.

Equality law

There are a number of strands of equality work that have their basis in law:

- Sex (gender) discrimination including gender re-assignment
- Race, ethnicity and culture
- Disability: defined as any substantial physical or mental impairment, that lasts, or is likely to last for more than twelve months and limits normal day-to-day activities
- Religion/belief including any clear belief system, not just organized religion, so it therefore covers atheists
- Sexual orientation
- Age

The most significant impact of the different equality laws is where a voluntary or community group employs staff. In the eyes of the law volunteers do not always have the same rights and protections as employees. However, as a volunteer manager, if you are offering training to volunteers or providing them with services or facilities several of the laws including the Disability Discrimination Act 1995, amended 2005 and the Sex Discrimination Act 1975, amended 2003 will apply to you. It's also unlawful to treat a volunteer, or potential volunteer less favourably because of their race, colour, ethnicity or nationality. Although the way equality legislation applies to volunteers is not always clear-cut the question remains; "Why would you discriminate against volunteers in any way that constitutes legally prohibited discrimination for employees?" In other words, regardless of the legal position, volunteers should have the right to equality.

What can volunteer managers do?

The concept of *'inclusive volunteering'* should not be a struggle nor onerous for volunteer managers. It does not require managers to accept all those who apply to volunteer. There are circumstances in which it would simply not be appropriate, or indeed legal; it is an offence to knowingly allow someone who has been convicted of a serious criminal offence to work with children. Inclusiveness is simply seeking to attract, recruit, welcome and engage with volunteers from all the eligible groups in your community.

The most obvious step is to create an equality statement. Though not required by law a policy or statement is good practice and is often asked for by funders. It is advisable to get volunteers involved in the creation or review of a policy; it promotes a sense of belonging, recognizes their value to the organization, and gets their buy-in from the outset. The policy should be written in plain English and should begin with a statement that acknowledges that some groups face disadvantages. And it should commit the organization to tackling discrimination. The policy should be a working document that sets targets, for example:

- To improve the organizations understanding of local demographics
- To encourage under-represented groups to volunteer; targeted recruitment of this nature is legally permitted to redress past inequality
- To Improve physical access for volunteers; organizations are legally required to make all reasonable adjustments
- To identify and remove barriers to volunteering wherever possible
- To provide training or support to volunteers, including those from disadvantaged groups.
- To record and monitor the gender, disability and race/culture of all volunteers and volunteer applications

Once the policy is written, agreed by volunteers - and any other group affected by it - and endorsed by someone senior in the organization volunteer managers should be aware of their own role in achieving the objectives set. There is a range of ways that volunteer managers might take forward equality work including taking into account religious holidays when you plan events and volunteer socials. To help with this (http://www.bbc.co.uk/religion/tools/calendar provides a multi-faith calendar.

The RAISE Equalities toolkit goes into more detail and suggests three levels at which inclusiveness can be implemented:

Psychological level
- Challenge the inappropriate views or comments of service users or other volunteers. It could be illegal not to challenge discriminatory remarks as it could contribute to the creation of intimidating or hostile environments for some volunteers.

- Provide awareness training to volunteers

- Uphold the organizations equality statement and principles; volunteer managers should be a good role model.

Practical level
- Seek to remove as many practical barriers as you are reasonably able to.

- Think about physical access to buildings and to the volunteering environment;

- Be flexible in the volunteering role you offer; can it be broken down or shared out to avoid an element that presents a barrier to some groups?

- Provide support for new volunteers that might include establishing a 'buddy system' with experienced volunteers

- Have regular one-to-one meetings, or check-ins, with volunteers to check if they need anything to help them fulfil their role

Political level	- Know the demographics of your local community; local authorities are a good source of information
	- Champion equality and inclusiveness within your organization
	- Make sure that volunteers are involved in the development and review of equality statements
	- Empower all of your volunteers
	- Ensure that any monitoring information collected from volunteers is reviewed and acted upon.

Simon, a severe dyslexic, contacted an organization he was keen to volunteer with. They sent him a mountain of paperwork and he was instantly put off. He later contacted the local healthy walking programme. The volunteer manager invited him in for a chat and offered to complete the paperwork with him over a coffee so removing the barrier. Sometime later, the volunteer manager asked Simon if he would like to take over as senior volunteer walk leader. The role had extra responsibility including writing rotas and Simon - who now trusted his volunteer manager - decided to tell them about his dyslexia. The volunteer manager simply asked what they could change in the new role to make life easier. They made some changes and Simon stayed in the role until the end of the project.

The first organization did nothing really wrong. They just had not thought through how they could be inclusive. The healthy walks project took simple steps like helping with paperwork and flexing a role description to include Simon. In return they had a committed and motivated volunteer.

It is not always possible to change a volunteer role and if you genuinely cannot find a way to fit a potential volunteer into your project be aware of what else is going on locally and help them find something that suits them so that you comply with the NOS for Volunteer Managers.

Some common questions

Should my equality policy target, or highlight, the groups I think face the greatest disadvantages in volunteering for us?

It can be tempting to start with a list of groups who might be disadvantaged in some way but it is generally not recommended. There is a good chance that one group will get forgotten and people may fit into more than one category. The term equality can be misinterpreted as giving everyone the same chances – equal rights. This is not the essence of inclusive volunteering. Inclusiveness means recognizing that all your volunteers are individuals and to get the best from them a volunteer manager should tailor any support or help to them individually. So when writing an equality policy it is far better to adopt the approach that all your organization respects the individuality of all your volunteers. In practical terms that might sound like a lot of work but in most cases it is just common sense and the willingness to take small actions - like offering to complete paperwork for your volunteers.

Can we recruit a volunteer who is disabled? Isn't it wrong for them to 'work' as a volunteer if they are on benefits because they are not fit to take on a paid job?

Those who receive benefits because they are long-term unable to work through sickness or disability and therefore in receipt of Incapacity Benefit are allowed to volunteer. Historically someone claiming Incapacity Benefit could only volunteer for a limited number of hours. However since the Social Security (Welfare to Work) Regulations (1998) this is no longer the case and there is no limit on the number of volunteer hours provided the volunteer work itself does not suggest the individual is capable of working. It would not be appropriate for a volunteer claiming a physical inability to work to be doing heavy gardening work or volunteering as a stage hand for a drama group. However there is no reason why they could not volunteer in less physical roles.

It is not unknown for volunteers in receipt of Incapacity Benefit to face problems. Volunteer managers might consider drafting a statement that highlights the distinction between work and the volunteering activities, particularly the flexibility of being able to commit to volunteering as the volunteers medical condition allows. It is also worth noting that Disability Living Allowance, Attendance Allowance and Severe Disablement Allowance are not affected by volunteering.

So how does the Disability Discrimination Act (DDA) apply to volunteering?

Whether the terms of the DDA apply to volunteers is not immediately obvious although the government has expressed a view that if necessary they will bring voluntary roles under the terms of the act. Either way it is good practice to apply the ethos of the act to your volunteers. As a volunteer manager you must not treat a disabled potential volunteer less favourably because of their disability. Volunteer managers must also make every *reasonable* adjustment to make their opportunity accessible to all sections of the community. What is deemed to be reasonable will depend on a variety of factors including - but not limited to - the size of your organization, the funds available to make adaptations, the specific demands of the volunteering role that cannot be changed and the nature of the building the group is based in. Local Councils for Voluntary Services (CVSs) can usually offer advice to groups (see Further Help).

Unemployment isn't an equality issue, is it?

Depending on their particular circumstances unemployed people can face various challenges to volunteering.

Kath had been out of work for 7 years. On her first day as a hospital volunteer she was terrified: "It had been so long since I'd been in a work situation, I didn't even know what to wear. I remember standing in the car park and I nearly didn't go in!"

Volunteers who have been unemployed for long periods of time might well struggle with confidence and that is something a good volunteer manager will be alert to. Other challenges can be far more practical. Most volunteering opportunities ask potential volunteers to provide references. Finding two references can be difficult if you have been out of work for a long time. Volunteer managers should seek other ways around this; reconsider who you will accept references from or recruit the volunteer in a supervised position for a specified period of time to allow them to prove themselves?

Paying out of pocket expenses is another important equality issue. It is good practice but some small community groups cannot afford to it so they present a barrier for those on a low income. If your organization can not pay expenses, volunteer managers should look for other ways around this barrier. Try asking your volunteers for their ideas! If you do pay expenses but only pay them monthly some people might find it difficult to pay their travel costs for a whole month before getting any of it back. It is worth noting that it is legally acceptable to pay expenses in advance provided that you get receipts and any change back from your volunteer. That can make life much easier for those on low incomes to volunteer.

Jamie faced an entirely different situation. The town cricket club he volunteered for offered expenses but none of the other volunteers claimed them. Most of them said they didn't want to take money from the club which made Jamie feel really uncomfortable claiming his, and he would often struggle on without asking for them.

There are several ways that the volunteer manager could have dealt with this. They could have offered to collect Jamie to save him paying out. Or they could have insisted that all volunteers claim expenses and said if they wanted to support the club they could donate the expenses back to the organization. Or the manager could remind the volunteers that not claiming expenses makes it look like the club is cheaper to run than it actually is and could misrepresent costs to potential funders.

Finally there are common misunderstandings around how many hours those on unemployment benefits may volunteer for. Anyone receiving Jobseekers' Allowance may undertake volunteering provided they continue to actively seek employment and remain available for paid work. It is good practice for volunteers to inform Jobcentre Plus of their intention to volunteer but there is no specified limit on the number volunteer hours they can do. However volunteering 'full-time' might suggest that the individual is not actually seeking employment. The rules allow residential volunteering for up to fourteen days provided the individual can still be contacted if a job becomes available. Similarly volunteers are entitled to 48 hours notice of the need to attend interview and do not have to start work immediately; a delayed start of one week is permitted.

We think we genuinely need a specific type of person – is this discrimination?

There are some circumstances where a number of groups might reasonably be excluded from a volunteering opportunity. A community group for Muslim women looking for an advice worker and a swimming teacher are legally permitted to advertise for a female swimming teacher and a female Muslim advice worker because of the requirements of their religion. This is known as a genuine occupational reason (GOR) however, there must be a real and substantial reason for excluding groups. More information on GOR can be found in "Making Equality Simple" by National Council for Voluntary Organisations (NCVO).

Exercise:

1. Do you know what your local community is like - who is out there - and do your volunteers really reflect the different groups within your community?

2. Does your organization have an equality statement that is written in plain English?

3. Were your volunteers involved in writing the statement or consulted about it?

4. Has the statement been agreed by senior members of the organization such as the trustees?

5. Is the statement mentioned in your mission statement and given out with volunteer recruitment information? And is it published to existing volunteers?

6. Do you make it clear that you welcome volunteer applications for all sections of your local community?

7. Is the statement reviewed to make sure you are living up to it?

8. Has someone in the organization or group been nominated to lead on making sure you are as inclusive as possible?

9. Do you provide equality training or information to your volunteers; this could be as simple as talks in meetings about disability awareness, or cultural awareness?

10. If the answers to any of the above is "no" write an action plan to redress the situation.

Five: Inductions & Developing Volunteers

Helping volunteers to find their feet and feel confident is identified in various aspects of the NOS and plays a big part in helping to retain people. It begins the moment they agree to join you, and should start with a useful induction.

Though there are no definitive guidelines about the amount of training volunteers should be offered, helping volunteers to fulfil their duties safely and effectively is identified in the NOS.

This chapter explores some of the issues around providing training for volunteers as well as the types of training you might consider and dealing with volunteers who refuse training.

Volunteer inductions

Like the interview the length of the induction process will depend partly upon the size of your organization. For small groups a chat over coffee might do the trick, in larger organizations it might be a more structured process of meetings with key workers that takes place over a few volunteering sessions. But inductions are essential as they are a key part of welcoming new volunteers. As a minimum they should include:

- tours of the venue that they will be based at including facilities, equipment, emergency evacuation procedures and routines,
- information about the organization and their role within it
- details of the volunteer agreement and other key policies and documents
- health and safety arrangements
- introductions to colleagues
- information about claiming expenses
- details of any trial periods and support structures for volunteers
- details of any social events volunteer or team meetings, and on-going training opportunities.

Given the volume of information you need to get across in a volunteer induction they can become rather tedious. I remember two particular inductions that I had – one where I was given copies of all the relevant policies to read on my own and another where I was given a map of the building and sent off to mark on it where the fire exits and alarms, toilets and so on were. You can guess which one I learnt more from! The last thing you want to do is bore your volunteers or send them running for the hills with fear of the responsibility on their first day. It is always worth remembering that adults learn and understand more when they are actively involved in finding out the information and the average adult has only a 20 minute attention span for passively receiving information. Consider writing a quiz for volunteers to complete on their first day – it's a much more interactive way of helping them to find crucial induction information.

Developing volunteers

For some volunteers part of their motivation is personal development (see Chapter 1). Learning new skills is a great fringe benefit to volunteering and can be a great marketing asset during recruitment. Personal development for volunteers does not have to just be about training; keeping a record of a volunteer's progress and achievements can be just as valuable.

Remember Lisa, who we left volunteering for the rugby club? As her confidence grew she became more and more involved with the club and even made significant contribution to the evaluation report the club had to produce about its lottery funded children's coaching scheme. That achievement was something Lisa was extremely proud of and she cited it on her CV as she started applying for jobs.

If you do provide training for volunteers they should only be offered training that relates to the role that they fulfil. A Bonfire Society steward could receive first aid training but should not be offered I.T. courses if their role does not bring them into contact with computers. In this instance I.T. training would be seen as a 'perk' and could be viewed as payment. This risks making the volunteer an employee, rather than a volunteer.

As well as making sure they are appropriate to the role volunteer managers must avoid attaching strings to training opportunities. An employment tribunal deemed that a national counselling organization had created a contract of employment with volunteers when they stipulated the cost of training would have to be repaid if a minimum number of volunteering hours were not completed. If you offer training to volunteers you should not impose any obligation on the part of the volunteer.

Training does not have to mean an expensive course. There are some instances, where for health and safety reasons identified in a risk assessment or for insurance purposes volunteers may need to attend a recognized training course.

Josie was asked to take up the role of head coach of a children's netball team having been an assistant for two years. She needed to upgrade her governing body coaching qualification and acquire an approved first aid certificate.

For other volunteer roles there may be cheaper alternatives. Shadowing a member of staff or another volunteer can be very effective and has the added benefit of showing faith in your existing volunteers. This type of 'on the job' coaching also allows you to be very flexible with the time and place that training is delivered.

Some common types of training for volunteers:

First Aid training	Safeguarding children training
Food hygiene courses	Data Protection Act training
Fire safety training	Protection of Vulnerable Adults (POVA)
Manual handling	Lone worker safety training
Visual Display Unit (VDU training)	

If an established course is your only, or preferred, option for your volunteers, then contact your local CVS as they are often able to offer low-cost training for voluntary groups. Many local community colleges run free basic skills courses (up to level 2) and the national awarding body NCFE offer a Level 2 qualification in volunteering appropriate to any volunteering role.

Some voluntary organizations have sought accreditation for the 'in-house' achievements and training of their volunteers. Citizens Advice is one example of this. Though the process obviously incurs costs in terms of time and resources there are benefits worth considering. The opportunity to get a formal award can be very attractive to some groups of potential volunteers (see Chapter 1). It can also have a positive effect on volunteers with low self-esteem and have a positive impact on the skill level of your volunteers.

If you decide to offer recognized qualifications or introduce accreditation for your volunteer training it needs to be carefully managed to avoid putting off potential volunteers who have had negative experiences of education. The Learning and Skills Council can advise on accessing external accreditation for your volunteers or consider developing your own internal award scheme.

Finally; volunteers can't be forced to undertake training but where safety is an issue, for example when using cutting equipment as part of a green gym or writing evacuation procedures for a community theatre, it is reasonable to require volunteers to be attend training. The crucial part in encouraging reluctant volunteers is letting them know why the training is necessary and what the benefits are but being prepared to negotiate on where and when the training takes place. The timing of training can be crucial – if it is outside 'normal' volunteering times it can be difficult for volunteers. You might have to consider providing child care or varying the times. If your volunteer still refuses important training, you might question how serious they are about volunteering and the on-going relationship you have with them (see Chapter 9).

Six: Managing Risks

All volunteer-involving organizations, no matter how big or small, have a moral and legal obligation to take care of their volunteers and the beneficiaries of their activity. And where a volunteer is to be working closely with children – defined as under 18 years of age - or vulnerable adults - defined as having a substantial learning or physical disability, physical or mental illness or substantial reduction in physical or mental capacity due to advanced age - volunteer managers must ensure an enhanced Criminal Records Bureau (CRB) check is undertaken.

Ensuring that health and safety procedures are adhered to and that risks are controlled are part of the on-going responsibilities of the volunteer manager (National Occupational Standards for Managing Volunteers). This chapter looks at some of the issues associated with managing risk in volunteering.

What the law says

If a volunteer, or a member of the public suffers harm as a result of volunteering activities, the organization could be liable for that harm and the victim eligible for financial recourse. In serious instances, an organization could be guilty of corporate manslaughter if management failures are shown to have caused someone's death (Corporate Manslaughter Act 2007).

Where volunteer-involving organizations have even one paid member of staff the Health and Safety at Work Act 1974 (HASAWA) and the Management of Health and Safety at Work Regulations 1999 (MHSWR) will apply. These laws place a general duty of care on organizations to protect those 'working' for them (including volunteers) and those who come into contact with the organization's work. This means that volunteer managers have a duty to be aware of and to minimise potential risks.

Where voluntary groups employ no staff their legal obligations differ. An adults' Sunday league football team where all roles - manager, coach, treasurer, and secretary - are undertaken by volunteers is not legally required to have a health and safety policy or to conduct risk assessments. However, even small groups and clubs have a duty to ensure that their volunteers are safe. Even having a simple statement that addresses some of the key risks is better than nothing and will probably suffice. In the case of the Sunday league football team that might simply be a requirement that coaches confirm the safety of equipment and pitches prior to use, ensure a first aider is on hand during training and matches and requiring all those transporting players to away games to have road-worthy vehicles. However, if the same club was a children's football team, different and more serious risks might exist - see the section on 'vulnerable groups' below - and a risk assessment would most certainly be advised.

Risk assessments

The MHSWR requires organizations employing staff to carry out risk assessments. Where the organization has five or more employees these assessments must be formally documented. Although not necessarily a legal requirement it is good practice for even small volunteer-involving groups to review and manage risks, particularly where volunteers are involved in activities that might be hazardous such as green gym volunteers using potentially dangerous equipment or volunteer expedition leaders who take groups into 'wild country'. Having the details of these reviews written down is good practice and serves as a constant reminder to managers and volunteers.

Although responsibility for conducting assessments might fall to a member of the management committee or a trustee in some groups volunteer managers take the lead. Undoubtedly a volunteer manager should have considerable input into the risk assessment of any tasks undertaken by their volunteers.

Conducting an assessment need not be complicated or difficult. The Health and Safety Executive (HSE) advocate the following approach. Firstly, list the potential risks to your volunteers. When considering the risks to volunteers, the role description (see Chapter 2) is a good place to start. It sets out the tasks and activities that volunteers are likely to be involved in. Consider each in turn and create a list of everything that could go wrong no matter how trivial or unlikely it seems. Remember, everyone thought that the Titanic was unsinkable until it sank! Once you have the list consider how likely each event is to happen with 1 being extremely unlikely and 5 being highly likely. Then, score each potential incident on the level of harm that could occur with 1 for something causing minor injury up to 5 possible death. Now multiply the two scores froe ach event together to give a numerical representation of the seriousness of the risk posed. Though not the only method of assessing risk this approach does enable volunteer managers to see which activities carry the highest risk and gives a priority list for addressing the most dangerous risks first. (See the example below).

Once identified and rated steps should be taken to remove or reduce the risks, particularly those with the highest scores. In legal terms the actions organizations are expected to take are balanced against the likelihood of harm occurring, the seriousness of the likely harm and the financial cost to the organization.

Commonly taken actions include:

- preventative, or protective actions include providing information or training such as manual handling training,
- changing the way things are done by, for example, providing equipment to lift and carry heavy equipment, or
- avoiding the activity altogether and this might be done by removing that activity from volunteer role descriptions or even stating that volunteers should not undertake that activity.

In addition, you might want to transfer the risk, by insuring against it. Usually, the most appropriate course is a combination of actions.

Finally, it is good practice to review risk assessments for volunteers regularly. The roles volunteers fulfil can change, the health and fitness of volunteers can vary and rules can get forgotten over time. An annual review date should be built into your assessment and the assessments should be revisited if the volunteer's role changes dramatically or if there is reason to suspect the original assessment is no longer valid.

Insurance

It is not unheard of for volunteers to cause or suffer injury in the course of their volunteering and in today's climate of litigation every organization that involves volunteers should have an insurance policy that covers volunteers. Volunteers are usually covered by the organization's employer's liability insurance or public liability (third party) insurance. In this sense the law does not distinguish between employees and volunteers although volunteers should be explicitly mentioned in policy documents. Employer's liability covers volunteers affected by accidents, diseases or injuries resulting from their volunteer work, whereas public liability covers members of the public who may suffer loss or harm following the actions of those representing your organization.

The Volunteer Managers Handbook

Extract from a sample risk assessment for a volunteer handy-person scheme undertaking repairs to homes of older people.

Hazard	Who is at risk?	How likely is the risk?	How serious would injury be?	Risk rating	Steps taken	Review date
Mobile lone worker	Volunteer	3	4	(3 x 4) 12	Mobile phones issued to volunteers Personal safety training Volunteer manager regularly checks on volunteers	Sept 11
Risk of injury to volunteers during maintenance work	Volunteer	4	5	20	Volunteers asked to complete an annual health screening questionnaire to identify increased risks Jobs risk assessed prior to starting First aid training and equipment given Jobs with greater risk attached (i.e.: at height) undertaken by minimum of two volunteers Personal Safety equipment provided	Sept 11
Injury caused by poor workmanship	Service beneficiary and general public	4	5	20	New volunteers' handy work supervised for 6 months Professional Indemnity Insurance	Jan 12

~ 65 ~

In instances where volunteers require a particular skill, like volunteer sports coaches, professional liability insurance might also be considered necessary. These policies provide cover against claims arising from inaccurate advice such as poor training drills and practices and unintentional breach of copyright or confidentiality.

Volunteer managers should ensure that insurers have been notified that volunteers need to be covered by the policy, particularly where a group has children or older volunteers, as some policies place limitations on the age of volunteers.

Children and vulnerable adults

Many volunteer-involving projects are designed to benefit children or vulnerable groups. Such individuals can be susceptible to abuse. Abuse may be noticed or perpetrated by volunteers. Volunteer managers must be equipped to deal with it. The flow chart on page 51 is a suggested template for dealing with disclosed or suspected abuse.

The NSPCC describe five types of abuse – physical, sexual, emotional, bullying and neglect - that can affect children. However, it should not be forgotten that older people are also at risk of abuse. It is estimated that up to 500,000 older people are being abused in England at any time and it is likely to be more common for those with dementia or communication difficulties. Elder abuse can be physical, psychological, sexual and neglect, but may also include financial abuse.

Ideally any volunteers that regularly come into contact with vulnerable groups should offered relevant training; either safeguarding children training or protection of vulnerable adults training – POVA. At the very least managers should ensure that volunteers are alert to some of the behavioural signs that might suggest abuse (see below) and their duty to report any suspicions or declarations of abuse. Knowing the procedure for this should be part of the volunteers' induction.

Some of the behavioural signs that might suggest possible abuse include but are not limited to:

- a lack of trust in individuals you would expect to see trusted,
- significant change in mood, personality or behaviour including becoming unusually withdrawn or aggressive,
- unexplained or untreated injuries,
- pain, itching or bleeding from the genital area,
- rapid change of physical appearance,
- refusal to remove clothing or change in front of others
- (in older people) sudden changes to their banking practices, or
- (in children) a level of sexual awareness inappropriate for their age.

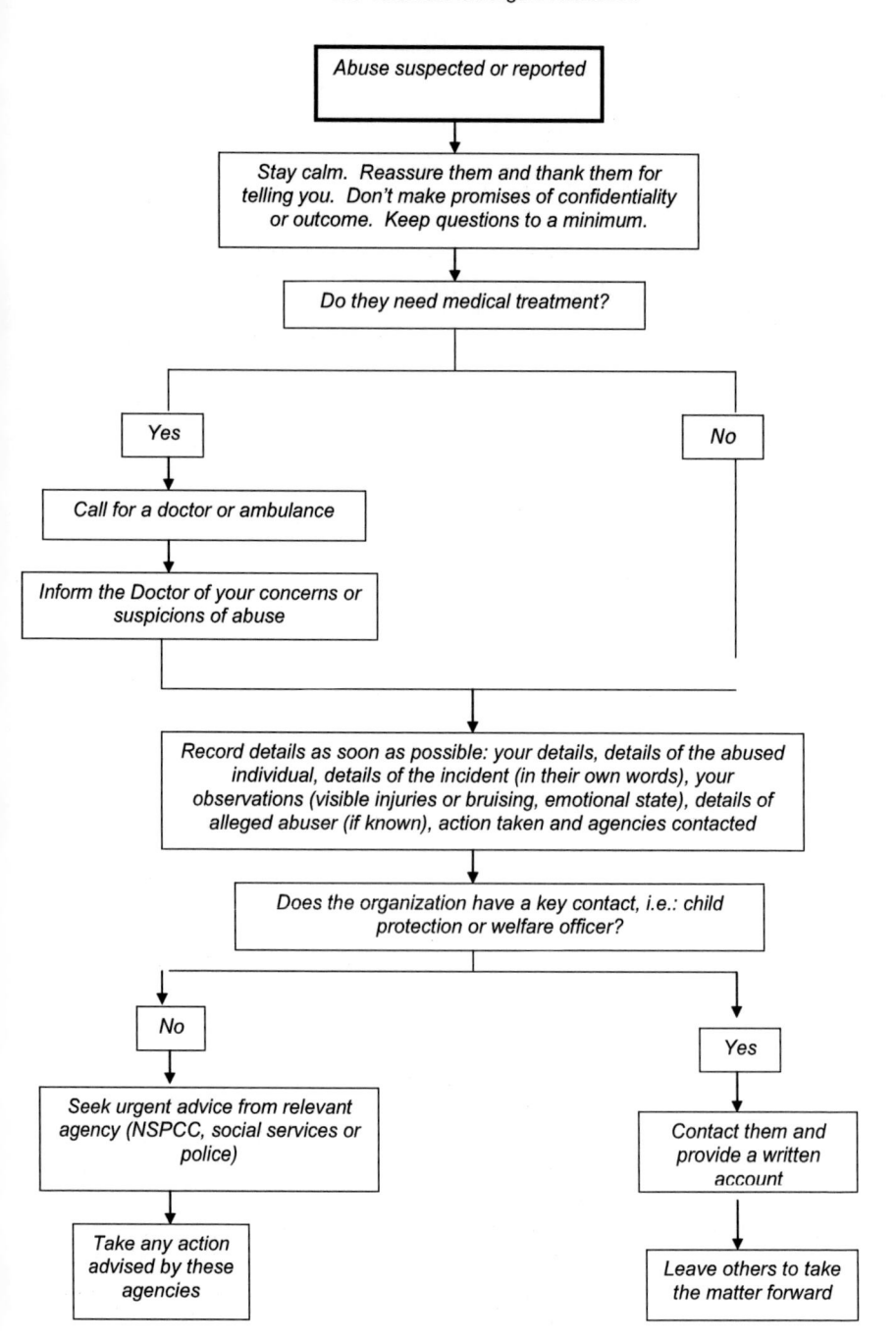

The Volunteer Managers Handbook

Abuse suspected or reported

↓

Stay calm. Reassure them and thank them for telling you. Don't make promises of confidentiality or outcome. Keep questions to a minimum.

↓

Do they need medical treatment?

- **Yes** → Call for a doctor or ambulance → Inform the Doctor of your concerns or suspicions of abuse
- **No**

↓

Record details as soon as possible: your details, details of the abused individual, details of the incident (in their own words), your observations (visible injuries or bruising, emotional state), details of alleged abuser (if known), action taken and agencies contacted

↓

Does the organization have a key contact, i.e.: child protection or welfare officer?

- **No** → Seek urgent advice from relevant agency (NSPCC, social services or police) → Take any action advised by these agencies
- **Yes** → Contact them and provide a written account → Leave others to take the matter forward

Unfortunately it is entirely possible that volunteers may be the perpetrators of abuse. Screening potential volunteers who will work with vulnerable groups using CRB checks and references is a central part of reducing these risks (see Chapter 4). Potential volunteers may come to your organization having already been CRB checked either for their work or for their last volunteering role. It can be tempting to re-use the previous disclosure form as evidence of their suitability. However 'portable' CRB disclosures carry risks and the concern of the volunteer manager should always be the safety of those the disclosure is designed to protect. As soon as a CRB check is issued, it is out of date. Any offence committed after the check is printed will not show and in some instances the law categorically requires new checks to be carried out (Protection of Children Act List, and the Protection of Vulnerable Adults List).

It should be remembered that CRB checks are not foolproof. Many of those convicted of abuse on vulnerable individuals had no relevant previous convictions. For this reason any volunteer managers placing volunteers with vulnerable people must consider other steps to minimize risks and have monitoring procedures in place. For example:

- a strict policy on references,
- a supervision period for new volunteers, where they are buddied with existing volunteers which also provides good support for new volunteers and values the experience of existing volunteers,
- a clear policy that volunteers are only to have contact with vulnerable groups whilst participating in the project and no personal contact beyond their volunteering is permitted,
- regular supervision with the volunteer manager as this increases the chance of volunteer managers noticing any problems.

If a CRB disclosure does reveal a criminal conviction in a potential new volunteer's past this does not necessarily prohibit that individual from volunteering with vulnerable groups. The Protection of Children Act (1999) and the Court Services Act (2000) makes it a criminal offence for an organization to knowingly allow a volunteer with a conviction for a 'serious' offence (murder, manslaughter, grievous bodily harm or rape) to work with children. But the situation with other offences is much more subjective. The volunteer manager should refer to the organization's policy on the recruitment of ex-offenders and consider the relevance, seriousness and date of any conviction(s) revealed. The manager should also consider any *pattern* of offending behaviour and the explanation offered by the potential volunteer. It is tempting to want to discuss the situation with a colleague but disclosing details of someone's criminal convictions to another without their consent is an offence under the Data Protection Act, and a breach of their human rights.

Once a volunteer manager has made a decision whether to accept or decline a potential volunteer the content of the disclosure is no longer relevant. In line with the Data Protection Act the details should only be kept as long as necessary. Volunteering England advocate that a period of time should be allowed for the potential volunteer to query or contest the decision and that after that the disclosure should be destroyed.

Finally; volunteers can be open to false allegations of abuse from service users. Volunteer managers should ensure that steps are taken to reduce the risk of this to protect their volunteers. Factors like the number and gender of volunteers, especially in sensitive environments like changing rooms, should be given special consideration in organizational policies. In these circumstances volunteer managers must ensure that clear guidelines exist about discipline, photographing or videoing 'performances' and what to do if a parent or carer does not arrive to collect a service user at the agreed time. Once guidelines exist managers must make sure they are communicated to volunteers, with regular reminders.

Other risks that volunteer managers should consider

Any volunteer-involving group that has responsibility for premises such as scout huts, community centres and sports club-houses, are legally obliged to take all reasonable steps to ensure the building and surrounds are safe. If an organization has employees the organization is bound to undertake a first aid assessment and ensure appropriate first aid is available. The content of first aid assessments will depend on the nature of the activity; coaching rugby is likely to have very different first aid issues than running a community arts project for young mothers. Where a group has no employees the group is not bound to conduct first aid assessments. But it is something that should be considered and when organizations hold public events, like bonfires, first aid provision must be made. Further information can be obtained from the Health and Safety Executive (see Further Help).

Managing volunteer drivers has a number of unique risks. A volunteer driver scheme that fails to undertake appropriate checks could be guilty of corporate manslaughter if someone dies as a result of a serious accident. Volunteer managers should check the volunteer's driving license at recruitment and occasionally throughout their volunteering. The license should be full and preferably free of endorsements. Some organizations enforce a minimum amount of driving experience although arguably this is discrimination. Is a young driver necessarily any less safe than any other driver? The volunteer manager should be reasonably sure of the vehicle's safety. Ask for evidence of an MoT if applicable, and ensure that seatbelts are working. A clear policy on the consumption of alcohol by volunteers should be in place; they should be advised not to have consumed alcohol for at least twelve hours before a journey. The level of motor insurance required, either third party or fully comprehensive, is at the discretion of the organization, but all volunteer drivers should inform their insurance company of their volunteering role. Volunteer Managers may provide volunteers with a template letter for this (see below). Failure to inform an insurance company could invalidate the volunteer's motor insurance. However, their volunteering role should not affect their insurance premium.

Volunteers name
Volunteers address

Date

Insurance company name
Insurance company address

Dear Sir/Madam

                Re: ***(Policy Number)***

I intend to undertake voluntary work and, from time to time, I will use my vehicle to carry passengers or to carry out other duties, as requested. I will receive a mileage allowance for these journeys to cover the running costs of my vehicle in accordance with Section 1(4) of the Public Passenger Vehicles Act 1981, which exempts me from both Passenger Service Vehicle and Hackney Carriage / Private Hire Car licensing laws.

I should be grateful if you would confirm that my existing policy covers me for such volunteer driving – please use the 'tear off' slip below. Please also confirm that my insurance policy contains a clause indemnifying the agencies with which I am a volunteer against third party claims arising out of the use of my vehicle for such voluntary work.

Yours faithfully

Volunteers name

This is to confirm that your insurance policy covers voluntary driving (for which a mileage allowance may be received). This also confirms that the above policy contains a clause indemnifying the agencies with which you are a volunteer against third party claims arising from the use of the vehicle on such voluntary work.

Insurance Company stamp:

Re (Policy Number):

Policy holders name:

Volunteer managers have 'control' over personal information about their volunteers. They are therefore bound by the principles of the data protection act and must not pass on information without an individual's consent. Where volunteers become privy to sensitive information about service users such as a befriending volunteer knowing about an individual's medical conditions it would not be unreasonable, nor likely to be considered contractual, to ask volunteers to sign a 'confidentiality pledge'. It is also fair to consider that a breach of confidentiality is grounds for cessation of the volunteering relationship (see Chapter 8).

Volunteers can be involved in 'lone working' where they volunteer in premises on their own, in remote locations or as mobile volunteers travelling to people's homes. Lone working can increase risks to volunteer safety. Wherever possible volunteer managers should seek to avoid volunteers being 'lone workers'; either by changing role descriptions or requiring activities to be undertaken by more than one volunteer. Where it cannot be avoided, lone working volunteers should be fully advised of the risks and how to mitigate them and adequately trained in first aid or with lone worker personal safety courses. They should be provided with relevant equipment - first aid kits, mobile phones, torches, personal safety alarms - and procedures should be in place to increase their safety, such as volunteer managers making regular telephone checks on them.

Managing risk is sometimes viewed as a burden, especially for smaller voluntary and community groups. However, it is crucial to protect organizations from potential litigation and a sign of the volunteer manager's commitment to ensuring the safety of their volunteers. Risk assessments do not have to be laborious and many of the steps taken to protect volunteers will be relatively simple.

Seven: Rewarding & Retaining Volunteers

Retaining volunteers is essential to the success of any ongoing volunteer-involving project and there is much that volunteer managers can do to influence retention and ensuring that volunteers are supported, motivated, developed and given feedback is central to the National Occupational Standards for Managing Volunteers. Volunteers are not tied to organizations in the same way that employees are so managers need to be more creative in the way they support and motivate their volunteers. Support and supervision is also a key mechanism for avoiding problems – when things go wrong volunteers often do not realize that they have done something wrong.

A simple and sincere 'thank you' means a lot to most volunteers. Regular supervision or informal chats are a simple way of thanking, motivating and consulting your volunteers.

Chapter 7 explores the benefits of supervision as well as some of the ways that volunteer managers can recognize and reward the contributions of their volunteers.

Volunteers have every right to expect to enjoy their role and to be supported in their volunteering. Ensuring that volunteers feel valued is part of the responsibility of the volunteer manager and goes a long way to help retain volunteers.

As a project manager for a county-wide support group for deafened adults, David found he spent a lot of his time on promoting the group to potential volunteers, interviewing and screening applicants and then inducting and training new volunteers. It wasn't until he attended a volunteer manager's workshop that he realized he didn't have a problem with recruitment; his challenge was keeping the volunteers that he'd worked so hard to get.

Retaining volunteers starts with the development of a good role description (see Chapter 2). Effective role descriptions seek to balance the more mundane tasks with the enjoyable activities and those that provide volunteers with the chance to own a piece of work. Taking the time to get to know potential volunteers and understand their motivations for volunteering is another simple step to increase volunteer motivation and retention (see Chapter 1). Volunteer managers should also make sure that they provide appropriate support and feedback - including thanks - to volunteers (National Occupational Standards for Managing Volunteers).

At the workshop David said that he was aware that many of his volunteers didn't stay with the group very long, and he had started giving them certificates in recognition of the number of hours volunteered, but with little success. He had convinced himself that that was the way things were - volunteers often didn't stay long. After the workshop, he looked again at the role descriptions and had to admit, some of them weren't very inspiring! After revamping the roles, when someone expressed an interest in volunteering with him, he took a few moments to understand what they wanted to get from volunteering. He was then honest about whether he could match their needs. With his existing volunteers he started offering informal supervision which ultimately highlighted the fact that some volunteers were angry about the certificates. They felt that rewarding the number of hours volunteered meant volunteers who could offer only a few hours a month were less valued. That is not to say that these steps revolutionized David's life over-night, but he certainly found within a few months that he was spending less time recruiting new volunteers and had built up a much stronger relationship with his existing team.

Supervising volunteers

Volunteers generally like to know that there is someone that they can turn to for advice and support and to whom they are able to express their feelings and thoughts. We all like to get feedback, to know whether we have done something well or not. Having 'supervision' with volunteers is one way of ensuring that the ethos of valuing volunteers is not just paid 'lip service' to. Even informal volunteers should be offered supervision or support. Sometimes it is easy to assume that everything is OK but the 'no news is good news' approach is not the best approach to valuing volunteers.

In volunteering supervision does not mean the same as supervision of employees. The bureaucracy involved in the latter approach is directly at odds with the informality that many volunteers are looking for. Supervision with volunteers is not an assessment either. The exact format of supervision should be appropriate to the volunteer's role but it should provide an opportunity for both sides to give and receive feedback. In this way, it can help you to identify and deal with any potential problems before they threaten the retention of volunteers.

A children's swimming club relies on several parents 'helping out' with transport to swimming galas. The arrangement had been working very well since the club began in 1998; all the parents were CRB checked and received a mileage allowance. Some parents had even continued to help after their own children had grown up.

Recently, two of the most reliable parents had become disaffected with the club and had stopped helping. They felt that the club leaders were not doing enough to ensure that the children respected and valued the volunteers and their cars.

Had those in charge of the club made sure they regularly checked with volunteers that everything was OK, these feelings might have been brought to light in time for the club to act before they lost their volunteers. Remember, not everyone is confident to complain about something – you may need to coax it out of them!

The mechanism for supporting volunteers varies hugely between organizations. Some common approaches include:

- peer support schemes with other volunteers
- an open door policy from the volunteer manager
- specific drop-in times when volunteers can visit their manager
- regular telephone calls to 'catch-up'
- scheduled monthly, quarterly or annual 1-2-1 meetings held in a private place
- a quick 'check-in' at the end of each session
- group meetings
- regular social events, where 'shop-talk' is likely to be a natural side-effect. These must be inclusive and take into consideration the needs of all volunteers such as dietary needs, family pressures and cultural issues
- a named contact to take problems to
- an annual survey of volunteers.

The choice of approach and the frequency of supervision should take into account the type of volunteering, how often the volunteer manager has direct contact with their volunteer, how long the volunteer has been with the organization, how well the manager feels the relationship is going and whether any concerns have been raised or highlighted.

Stewards at annual bonfire celebrations are volunteering at one-off event but feedback should still be sought. A quick phone call after the event or a coffee with them to see if they enjoyed the experience or need anything else from you, like a reference, is probably all that is warranted; but do it. For long-term volunteers there is more likely to be regular meetings with the volunteer manager. These should be an informal two-way conversation about how well things are going. A template for face-to-face supervision is shown below. Whether or not the details of these are formally recorded is a matter of choice for the volunteer manager; but if they are taken records should be stored securely.

Whichever way the volunteer manager decides to support their volunteers it should be explained to volunteers as part of the induction process.

Template for a volunteer supervision meeting.

Volunteer Name:	
Meeting Date:	

Since we last met, how have things been? What has gone well? Are you still enjoying the role?

Has anything not gone as well as you would have liked?

Are you enjoying working alongside the other volunteers / staff?

Have you had any problems with, or got any suggestions about any of our policies?

Is there anything else in the organization that you would like to get involved with?

Have you noted anything you feel you would like training or support with?

Are you getting everything you need from me as a volunteer manager?

Is there anything else you'd like to raise or suggest?

Motivating and recognizing volunteers

Volunteers generally want much the same thing as the rest of us – to feel valued, respected, useful and part of the team. There are many different ways to recognize and motivate volunteers, and volunteer managers may adopt a mix and match appropriate to valuing their volunteers. However, understanding your volunteers is fundamental to effectively appreciating their work. Some volunteers enjoy public recognition whilst others would find it embarrassing or even harrowing. A good volunteer manager will know enough about their volunteer's character to assess this. However, every project is likely to have a mix of volunteers and a singular approach to thanking volunteers is not always the best. It is absolutely appropriate for a recognition system to be made up of a mixture of different types of formal and informal rewards. Below is a list of just some of the opportunities to value and motivate volunteers:

- Thank you letters or postcards
- Reimbursing out of pocket expenses
- Offering letters of reference or commendation
- Telling members of staff especially managers how great your volunteers are - in their presence
- Including volunteers on organizational structure charts
- Recognizing their good work in staff newsletters
- Delegating project work and giving volunteers ownership of tasks
- Giving badges, t-shirts, photographs and other souvenirs
- Acknowledgement in newsletters or at committee meetings
- Sending them Christmas cards
- Celebrating their birthdays
- Providing lunch at meetings
- Formal award ceremonies
- Celebration events or end of season volunteer socials
- Complementary membership of your organization

- Mentions in the local media
- Discount schemes – with your organization, or with partners
- Relevant training courses
- Certificates
- Long service awards
- Nominations for volunteering awards – see Further Help for details of some national awards or contact local authorities, local county sports partnerships or CVSs for information on local awards.

Some of these are explored in more detail below.

Delegating tasks Consider the types of tasks that could be delegated to volunteers that aren't currently. If a volunteer is seeking development and a challenge (see Chapter 1), taking on extra responsibility can be very motivating. However when offering new tasks to volunteers, managers should take into account the availability of the volunteer, their expectations, skills, needs and motivations. Getting this wrong is one of the quickest ways to de-motivate a volunteer. If you decide to delegate, communicate what is expected clearly as everyone finds their role easier if they understand what they are required to do, to what standard and by when.

Out of pocket expenses No-one should have to pay to volunteer. Volunteers give their time, which has considerable financial value, so refunding out of pocket expenses should be part of every volunteer-involving project and costs should always be built into budgets and any funding applications. Offering out of pocket expenses demonstrates that you value your volunteers and volunteers tend to think well of organizations that offer to reimburse their expenses.

The expenses you reimburse are a matter of choice for each organization and clearly dependent upon budget. As a general guide, travel costs to and from and during volunteering, meals and refreshments, care of dependents, postage, phone calls and the cost of any specialist clothing should be covered wherever possible. Travel expenses for volunteer rangers to get around countryside stations, training equipment for sports coaches, or the cost of refreshments for volunteer health walk leaders are all specific examples of where expenses are reimbursed.

It is reasonable to put limits on volunteer expenses and to ask volunteers to use the cheapest, accessible form of transport. Remember you are only reimbursing 'out of pocket' expenses. Anything over the actual cost incurred could be seen as payment. If volunteers are deemed to be receiving payment they will be liable for taxation and they could be seen as employees, with legal entitlements to national minimum wage, statutory sick pay and other basic employment rights. For that reason emphasise to your volunteers that they must provide receipts wherever possible and use the Inland Revenue guidelines for mileage (table 2). Though it might seem simpler avoid giving flat rate payments such as "£10 a day for lunch" as the rate may exceed the actual costs incurred by your volunteer.

Approved maximum mileage rates for travel expenses. Correct at the time of publishing. For current information visit www.hmrc.gov.uk/rates/travel.htm

	Rates for the first 10,000 miles
Cars and Vans	40p per mile
Passengers (giving a lift to another volunteer, or member of staff)	5p per passenger, per mile
Motorcycles	24p per mile
Bicycles	20p per mile

Some volunteers may take the view that accepting expenses is taking funds away from a charity and so refuse them. Volunteer managers must remember that payment of expenses is an equal opportunities issue. Though a commendable viewpoint, not everyone can afford to volunteer if their costs are not reimbursed. Allowing some volunteers to refuse to draw expenses risks leaving those who do take them feeling stigmatized. If a volunteer really does not want expenses suggest that once the payment is received they could donate the funds to a charity or back to the project.

There remains some confusion over who can receive expenses and whether it might affect state benefits. Volunteers who are asylum-seekers or are receiving state benefits can still receive expenses provided they do not exceed the actual expenditure. Where 'income' is received from expenses claimants may lose part of their benefits.

Remember, some volunteers might not have bank accounts so have provision to pay expenses in cash. Many groups deal with expenses monthly but managers should recognize that this might cause problems for volunteers on tight budgets. It is also worth noting that under the Social Security Amendment (Volunteers) Regulations 2001 Act volunteers on state benefits can receive expenses in advance, provided that any unspent money is returned and receipts are collected.

Formal rewards and recognition Any programme introduced to value your volunteers must fit with the type of volunteer and their values (see Chapter 1). Formal reward structures are most suited to those who seek community or peer approval for their work, but are irrelevant, and sometimes disliked, by those whose primary aim is helping others (see the example below). Similarly, long-service awards might be appropriate to stalwart volunteers but will not suit stepping stone or project hopper volunteers whose contribution is equally valuable. Stalwart volunteers often appreciate recognition from within the organization or presentations from authority figures. Stepping stone and project hopper volunteers benefit more from immediate and 'take away' rewards like certificates, photographs or other souvenirs.

> *The steering group of a leisure project were discussing ways to thank their volunteers. The project co-ordinator suggested a badge or certificate scheme. The reaction of one of the volunteers who was a member of the steering group surprised the co-ordinator. Not only was the volunteer adamantly opposed to a formal recognition scheme but they were angered by the suggestion.*
>
> *In this instance, the volunteer was a stalwart volunteer, highly intrinsically motivated. They genuinely felt that funds should only be spent directly on the beneficiaries. Recognition like simple 'thanks', or Christmas and birthday cards was all this volunteer wanted.*

Events Annual events, like volunteer parties and club socials are often seen as a good way of thanking your volunteers. If you decide to opt for this approach make sure they are inclusive for all volunteers. Some volunteers may have special dietary needs, or may not want to go to pubs for religious reasons. Check the date of the event does not clash with any key festivals for cultures other than your own and do not forget to invite any volunteers who have left you part way through the year or the project.– you never know, they might even be tempted to come back.

Training events Encourage and support your volunteers to attend relevant training events (see Chapter 5) to get qualifications. Investing in their skills shows you value them as part of the team. As well as the obvious courses for volunteers, like first aid courses or computer training, the National Council for Further Education (NCFE) offers a Level 2 Certificate in Volunteering. Some local training providers may be able to offer this course funded for volunteers. See Further Help for details of the NCFE.

But remember volunteers cannot receive payment. Schemes that 'pay' volunteers are inadvertently risking creating a contract of employment and 'payment' does not only relate to financial gain. It can refer to a number of 'fringe' benefits that projects give volunteers. Although offering training is an important part of a volunteering relationship, the training must be relevant to the work. To offer I.T. training to an event steward who has no need for computer skills could be deemed to be payment.

Gifts Volunteer managers also need to be careful of giving gifts. One-off gifts or payments, sometimes know as 'honoraria' are acceptable, but if there is a suggestion that it is a regular occurrence,, for example race marshals being given a bottle of wine after each race, it may become an expected 'perk' of volunteering. It could therefore be classed as payment and begin to indicate that your volunteers are paid.

Supporting and rewarding volunteers is an essential part of volunteer management and, if done appropriately, will improve volunteer retention. Managers should think carefully about the nature of the project and the types of volunteers. Supervision is essential but doesn't have to be overly formal and any reward or recognition scheme should value all volunteers. It can be too easy to identify your 'high profile' volunteers or those you have the strongest relationship with whilst forgetting others. Whatever approach a manager adopts to thank volunteers it doesn't have to cost a lot of money; a simple 'thanks' after each session costs nothing.

Exercise:

1. *In what ways do you currently 'supervise' your volunteers?*

2. *Can you do anything to improve two-way communication with volunteers?*

3. *Look at the list of ways to formally and informally reward volunteers, add any more that you can think of then identify those that would suit your volunteers and their particular motivations and needs.*

Eight: Dealing with Problems & Ending Relationships

Most volunteering relationships are enjoyable and benefit both the volunteer and the organizations. Occasionally things don't go smoothly. I have encountered volunteers arriving at their organization intoxicated, engaging in public arguments with other volunteers and even displaying behaviour that borders on sexual harassment. When things like these happen it can be really difficult for volunteer managers to know what to do. Can you reprimand a volunteer? What rights do volunteers have to complain, if they are unhappy?

And what about ending volunteering relationships? The focus of attention for many volunteer managers is upon initiating volunteering and recruiting volunteers but the other end of the relationship warrants consideration too. Whether it's the end of a project's funding, the volunteer simply wants to move on, or your parting is less than amicable, ending the relationship appropriately is crucial for volunteer managers. After all, this is the last impression your volunteer has of you. This final chapter looks at ways of dealing with problems and the end of a volunteer relationship.

The steps in this book are designed to help volunteer managers avoid problems. If clear reasons for involving volunteers were identified from the start, an appropriate role description was created, a good match of volunteer to role was made and clear expectations were made by both parties during inductions, then problems are less likely. Unfortunately, sometimes problems in volunteering relationships do still arise and regular catch-up meetings with volunteers are the key to catching them early (see Chapter 7).

Failing to notice a change in motivation for the volunteer is a classic problem for volunteer managers who fail to regularly check in with volunteers. Over time a volunteer's needs can change, especially if a particular need has been met. Common problems, like poor time-keeping, not turning up for agreed sessions or taking on tasks that they are not supposed to might suggest that volunteers are no longer satisfied in the role they fulfil. If this is the case it is time to explore other roles the volunteer could undertake. In smaller organizations opportunities may be limited but the volunteer manager should still be willing to support their volunteer to develop, even if this means them moving on to another organization. Remember this is a normal characteristic of some types of volunteer. (see Chapter 1).

If a problem does escalate or the issue is more serious then having a clear process for resolving problems is not only good practice but provides a safety net for handling situations with confidence. The process does not have to be complex or lengthy but in the interests of fairness and consistency it should be noted down and available to anyone to see.

Where an organization has volunteers and employees it is worth noting that a complaints and grievance policy for staff should not be applied to volunteers. Employees have certain legal rights based in employment law, bestowing these upon volunteers by having a single policy could begin to suggest that volunteers are viewed as staff.

It can be helpful to set out in your problem-solving document (or in the organization's code of conduct) details of any actions that would lead to instant dismissal of a volunteer. For example, theft, acts of violence or aggression, deliberate falsification of documents (including expenses claims), harassment or other gross misconduct.

The thought of disciplining volunteers does not sit comfortably with the flexible, welcoming image of volunteering. However, voluntary does not mean unprofessional and the organization has a right to strive for certain standards; after all your reputation or the safety of others could be jeopardized by inappropriate behaviour from volunteers. Volunteer managers are perfectly within their rights to issue verbal and written warnings to volunteers if appropriate.

Template for problem solving in volunteer-involving organisations

Our approach to resolving problems with our volunteers
It is our intention to protect our volunteers and the reputation of our organization. As an organization we are committed to resolving any problems or difficulties faced by our volunteers fairly, quickly and with respect for confidentiality.

The volunteer raises a problem	There is a problem with the volunteer
All our volunteers have the right to complain if they feel they have been treated unfairly by a member of staff, another volunteer, the organisation, the volunteer manager or a service user.	Sometimes problems can arise during the course of volunteering. We aim to be able to identify and resolve these as part of regular supervision with volunteers. Where a problem cannot be resolved informally, we will ensure that all volunteers facing discipline have the right to know why they are being disciplined and to put their case.
Step 1 Discuss the problem with the volunteer manager (if the complaint is about the manager, refer to another senior member of the organization). Volunteers may bring a friend if they wish. Notes should be taken of any agreement reached. If the problem cannot be resolved progress to step 2.	**Step 1** The volunteer manager will discuss the problem with the volunteer and identify actions to address the problem (this may include reminding volunteers of ground rules or policies, providing training or extra support). Take notes should be taken of both points of view, any agreements reached and a date for review. Where the issue persists, or a problem is more serious progress to Step 2.
Step 2 Submit a written complaint to _____ within ____ weeks of the problem arising. The organization will respond to the complaint within ___ weeks, and the outcome of any decision will be given to the volunteer immediately. If the volunteer is unhappy with step 2, they should progress to step 3.	**Step 2** The volunteer manager may provide the volunteer with a written warning detailing the problem. Volunteers may wish respond to the warning, by putting their case. If they wish to do so they should contact _____ within ___ weeks.
Step 3 Volunteers may appeal to the Chair of the management committee / trustee board. A volunteer may ask a friend to help with this. The management committee commit to respond to complaints within ___ weeks.	**Step 3 – last resort** Where this procedure has been followed and no solution has been found, or in cases of extreme misconduct on the part of the volunteer, the organization may dismiss the volunteer. This action will only be taken as a last resort and written details will be given to the volunteer.

	Appeal *Although volunteers are not covered by employment law rights to appeal, we recognise that some volunteers may wish to appeal against dismissal or disciplinary action.* *This can be done by contacting the Chair of the management committee /trustee board.*

Dismissing a volunteer

Having to ask a volunteer to leave is one of the hardest tasks that a volunteer manager may face, and it may not always be as straightforward as misconduct on the part of the volunteer.

The volunteer manager of a family support group faced the unenviable task of dismissing an older volunteer who had been with the organization for over 30 years. Although there is no reason to dismiss a volunteer simply because of their age, if they become unable to fulfil the role safely and effectively it may be time for them to leave. The ideal situation is to find a different role for them in the group, but sometimes that just isn't feasible. In the case of the family support group volunteer they had come to rely on the organization for their own social support and the services of other volunteers were being diverted to care for them. The only option for the manager was to be frank. Since no other roles existed in their organization he offered to help the volunteer move on to another group and made sure that the commitment they had given to their group over the years was celebrated. He even made sure they were invited back for volunteer socials from time to time.

The only other important thing for volunteer managers to note in relation to older volunteers is to confirm with their insurance companies whether their policy has age restrictions.

Where the problem-solving process has been followed and resolution has not been achieved it may be necessary to consider dismissing a volunteer. At this point many volunteers will leave the organization of their own accord. If a volunteer manager does need to dismiss a volunteer, it should be done in person. The meeting should be private, quick and professional. Expect the volunteer to react but do not get drawn into emotional conversations – a dismissal is not a two-way conversation. The meeting should be followed up with a letter to ensure that the reasons for the dismissal have been understood and describing any right to appeal. Finally, make sure that other members of the organization are aware that the volunteer is no longer with you – but remember that the reasons for the dismissal should be confidential.

Problems are not always with the volunteers

In organizations where paid staff and volunteers work side-by-side it is not unusual for problems to arise between the two. Employees can genuinely feel threatened by volunteers, believing them to be replacing employees or difficult to get rid of if they are 'not up to the job'. Conflict of this type makes for an unpleasant atmosphere and undermines the efforts of the manager to make volunteers feel valued and part of the team.

Alicia's experience was, unfortunately, not uncommon. Alicia was a hospital volunteer. She took the role after her mother had received such great care at the unit and was excited about being able to give something back to them. Sadly, the staff on the ward felt that it was much quicker to do the tasks themselves rather than show Alicia. Especially as a number of recent volunteers had left after only a short time. Their perception of volunteers was that they would not last so there was little point investing in them. After a couple of weeks of feeling like a burden Alicia left the hospital and the volunteer manager did not offer an exit interview or ask why she was leaving. So that pattern was probably repeated over and over.

Whenever volunteers and employees work side-by-side getting the staff motivated to accept volunteers is crucial to success. Volunteer managers should encourage a positive image of volunteering as a method of strengthening the work done by paid staff – not replacing it. Employees may need to be reassured that they (and the volunteer) will be supported to ensure that the relationship is a fruitful one and that problems with the agreement will be addressed promptly and fairly.

Ending relationships without problems

Not every volunteering relationship comes to an end acrimoniously. Sometimes volunteers are just ready to move on. There are a number of reasons why volunteers decide to cease volunteering:

- they had only volunteered for the run of a show, or for a sporting season (project hoppers);
- as parents they only wanted to volunteer whilst their children were involved (project hoppers);
- they achieved their target of getting into a paid post (stepping stone);
- they feel that they have got too old, or have become unwell and can no longer fulfil the role;
- they are students who only volunteered during their summer break;
- they are a stalwart volunteer who feels that they have 'done their share'.

Whatever the reason your volunteer has for moving on it is good practice to have an 'exit interview'. It is an opportunity for the volunteer to say where they felt supported - or where things could be improved - and a perfect chance for you to thank them. Like many aspects of volunteering, this can be done informally – a chat over coffee - or as a questionnaire given to the volunteer.

1. The things they enjoyed most about their volunteering role.

2. The things that they enjoyed least during their volunteering.

3. How well they felt accepted by staff, other volunteers and the organization as whole.

4. Did they get all the support they needed to help them volunteer?

5. Did they receive all the information that they wanted about the organization.

6. Was their induction process helpful? Can they suggest any ways to improve it?

7. How well did the role they undertook match the role description that they had been given?

8. Was the role interesting and enjoyable? Can they suggest any ways to improve the role?

9. Did they feel valued and appreciated by the organization and the volunteer manager?

10. Would they recommend volunteering with the organization to a friend?

As a volunteer leaves an organization it is a good idea to agree whether they would like a reference and possibly even the nature or content of the reference. Volunteer managers should also confirm with the volunteer what will happen to personal information that the organization holds about them. Remember, the Data Protection Act requires that information is not held longer than necessary, so if you are not going to offer a reference do you really need to keep their details? If not, make sure that the information is destroyed or disposed of securely.

If volunteer management is done well problems with volunteers are unusual and their contribution to voluntary and community projects can be phenomenal. Committed volunteers are amazing people, and though I may have encountered the odd problem along the way, I have never regretted my time spent working with them!

References

Big Lottery Fund. (2007) *Making a BIG difference: Annual Review 2006-2007*

Connors, T. D. (ed). (1997). *The Nonprofit Handbook*. Second Edition. John Wiley and Sons Inc; New York

Luks, A. and Payne, P. (1992). *The healing power of doing good: The health and social benefits of helping others.* Faw

McCurley, S. and Lynch, R (1994). *Essential Volunteer Management.* Directory of Social Change; London

National Council for Voluntary Organisations (2006). *The UK Voluntary Sector Almanac 2006: The State of the Sector.*

National Council for Voluntary Organisations (2007). *The UK Voluntary Sector Almanac 2007.*

Neuberger, J. (2008). *Volunteering in the Public Services: Health and Social Care.*

Regional Action and Involvement South East (RAISE). (2008). *Equalities Toolkit.*

Restall, M. (2005). *Volunteers and the Law.* Volunteering England; London

Volunteering England. *Employer supported volunteering – the guide.*

UK Workforce Hub. (2008) *Management of Volunteers – National Occupational Standards.*

Organisations and websites

Association for Volunteer Managers
www.volunteermanagers.org.uk

National Council for Voluntary Services
www.ncvo-vol.org.uk

Child Protection in Sport Unit.
NSPCC National Training Centre,
3 Gilmour Close,
Beaumont Leys,
Leicester, LE4 1EZ.
Tel: 0116 234 7278
www.thecpsu.org.uk

UK Workforce Hub
Tel: 020 7520 2490
www.ukworkforcehub.org.uk

Community Service Volunteers (CSV)
Tel: 0800 284533
www.csv.org.uk

Volunteer Development Agency Northern Ireland
www.volunteering-ni.org

Health and Safety Executive
Rose Court,
2 Southwark Bridge,
London,
SE1 9HS
Tel: 0845 345 0055,
www.hse.gov.uk

Volunteer Development Scotland
www.vds.org.uk

Institute of Volunteering Research
www.ivr.org.uk

Volunteering England (VE)
www.volunteering.org.uk

Learning and Skills Council
Tel: 0870 900 6800
www.lsc.gov.uk

Volunteering Ireland
www.volunteeringireland.com

National Centre for Volunteering.
www.volunteering.org.uk

Volunteering in the Third Age (VITA)
www.wrvs.org.uk/vita/home.htm

Volunteering Wales
www.volunteering-wales.net